Sheffield United

Illustrating the Greats

Text copyright 2006 © M Liversidge
Illustrations copyright 2006 © G Mackender, A Currier.

ISBN 1-905278-03-9
Printed in 2006 by Pickard Communication

The rights of Michael Liversidge as author of this work has
been asserted by him in accordance with the Copyright,
Design Patent Act 1988.

All rights reserved.
No part of this publication may be reproduced, stored in a
retrieval system, or transmitted, in any form or by any
means electronic, mechanical, photocopying, recording or
otherwise, without the prior permission in writing of the
copyright holder or publishers.

Published & Printed by Pickard Communication,
10-11 Riverside Park, Sheaf Gardens, Sheffield S2 4BB
Telephone 0114 275 7222 or 275 7444
Facsimile 0114 275 8866
email info@pickardcommunication.co.uk
www.pickardcommunication.co.uk

Introduction

Sheffield United started life as a cricket club. It was the need to keep players fit in the winter that led them to join the recently formed football league in 1892. Unfortunately for United, quite a few cricket/football teams had organised themselves and made the same decision to get elected to the burgeoning league. The governing body of the day deemed it had too many teams and formed a second division to which Sheffield United were elected.

United, who needed to succeed or return to being a cricket club, played one season in Division Two. They immediately gained promotion to the top flight of English football. Many years later, it was cricket that was to be deemed too costly to survive.

After their promotion, United, were possibly the premier club in the country. During the following seven years, they won the League championship in 1898 and lifted the FA Cup on two occasions 1899, 1902. The were also runners up in the league on two occasions in 1897 and 1900, and FA Cup runners up in 1901, losing to Spurs when the FA Cup went south for the first time.

For the next 13 years, until the First World War brought an end to domestic football, United were generally placed mid table. They did have four top six finishes but never really challenged for the Championship.

In 1915, the last season of full league and cup fixtures before the Great War, Sheffield United, gave their supporters a memorable tonic by winning the FA Cup with a victory over, today's money club, Chelsea. At a time when the horrors of the war in Europe were being made public in Britain, any cause for celebration must have been very welcome indeed.

After the War, United carried on in the same vein, mid table, occasionally reaching the top five but never challenging for Championship honours. Season 1924-1925 was a beacon for the Blades and Tunstall's only goal gave United a 1-0 Wembley win over Cardiff City. This was to be the last major honour Sheffield United were to win. Another nine years in the top division gave way to a bottom of the table performance in 1934 and relegation. United soon bounced back within five years but unfortunately Europe was becoming embroiled in another World War and domestic football was suspended again. During this conflict, Bramall Lanes John Street Stand was destroyed by 10 bombs in December 1940. The late forties and early to mid fifties were almost as up and down for United as Sheffield Wednesday (the Yo Yo club). During this time a certain legend called, Jimmy Hagan, graced the Blades team.

The late fifties, sixties, and early to mid seventies were halcyon times with some brilliant results, Arsenal, Manchester United, Spurs were all beaten and the odd double over Sheffield Wednesday did not go amiss. They reached the dizzy heights of the top of the first division, albeit for only a few weeks at the beginning of the season, and not at the end. Some outstanding players came to the fore in this period: Hodgkinson, Shaw G, Coldwell, Richardson, Shaw J, Summers, Badger, Jones, Birchenall, Gil Reece, Len Alchurch, to name but a few. Derek (Doc) Pace with a remarkable scoring record of over 175 goal in 302 appearances in all competitions was a joy to behold, good in the air and lightning fast over the 5 or 6 yards where it mattered. Tony Currie possibly the most influential Sheffield United player since Jimmy Hagan, was signed from Watford for, what is now an unbelievable fee of, just over £26,000. Alan Woodward scored double figures in 11 of out of 12 full seasons with the Blades. The other occasion was the relegation season of 1968 when only Gil Reece reached double figures.

The late seventies and early eighties saw a dramatic downsurge in fortune and a humiliating drop through all the divisions. Fortunately, new scoring sensation Keith Edwards, (35 league goals in 41 league games), helped united secure the 4th Division Championship. With another three promotions and one relegation in the 1980s United found themselves back, where they belong, in the top flight in 1990. However, after only four seasons at this level, two of them in the newly conceived Premiership, they sufferred relegation, again.

Since that shock to the system, United have forged themselves into, possibly, the top club in the country, outside of the premiership. They are solvent, have players who many teams covert, possess a manager who loves the club and not the salary, as is usually the case. The club seem to battle their way through to quarter and semi final places of both major cups with stunning regularity. They have been in play off positions three times now, without success, but it is surely coming. This year, 2006, possibly, probably, obviously.

Up the BLADES!

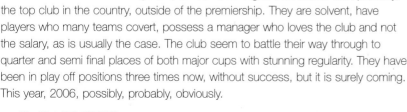

Contents

Contents *continued*

Sheffield United

Illustrating the Greats

Sheffield

William (Fatty) **Foulke** (also spelt Foulk or Foulkes)

William Henry Foulke was born April 12, 1874 in Dawley, Shropshire or Blackwell, Derbyshire. It depends on where you get your information. Some 20 years later he made his debut for Sheffield United.

A larger than life character, in more ways than one. William was said to have played for Sheffield United Football Club in a league championship winning season and three FA Cup finals at weights close to 20 stone. He also played one game at international level for England, without conceeding a goal, presumably at about the same weight. Although a tall man, six feet two inches, he must have been very overweight. In January 1895 he was at the more lithe weight of 14stone 5 lbs, so maybe he was not as large, weight wise, in some of those games as we are led to believe.

A last mention of Bill's weight, it states in *"100 Sheffield United Greats"* by Dennis Clarebrough that Foulkes was over 22 stone when he was transferred to Chelsea. They definitely got their monies worth.

Football was a vastly different game in those days. A goalminder or goalkeeper would do a very different job to today's custodians. Clearances and interceptions were mostly made with their feet. Let's be fair, who would want to go into a 50-50 tackle with Foulkes? Diving saves and sliding out at the opposition players feet weren't in the manual of the goalkeeping art in those early years. It was a more positional game and the keeper was more of a last man sweeper.

The fact of the matter is Foulkes was a very competent keeper. He won League Championships, FA Cup winners and runners up medals plus England international honours. This record confirms his ability and explains why he came to the attention of the England Selection Committee. No goalkeeper could have been carried through such an excellent series of results.

So, no matter what perceptions we have when seeing pictures of a large man, not looking as we expect the last line of defence to appear, the proven facts and many honours he won show just how good Bill must have been for Sheffield United, a club he played over 350 games for. He was also one of the best known and feared players of his generation, appearing on many postcards, cigarette cards. Such was his fame that his portrait appeared on the 1902 cup final programme when Sheffield United played Southampton, at Crystal Palace. Now that is an honour!

Foulkes was a big player in every sense and he seemed to attract the attention of the public and media of the day, like a magnet. Some newspapers would state he lifted this player or hurled that player over the touchline or into the crowd. Or in one case collided with an opposition player knocking him unconsious. He proceeded to pick him up by his shirt and carry him, one handed, to the touchline for treatment. It is also said of Foulkes that he could become agitated with members of the crowd. On more than one occasion he leapt over the barriers and went in hot pursuit of supporters who he thought had gone too far with their goading.

Bill was also a very good cricketer playing four first class matches for Derbyshire County Cricket Club in 1900.

After his retirement from football, Foulkes came back to Sheffield. He ran a public house, owned a grocer's shop and was a well respected gentleman. Unfortunately, he was only 42 years old when he died in a Sheffield nursing home in May 1916. Sclerosis of the liver being cited as the major cause of his demise on his death certificate. I believe William is buried in Burngreave Cemetery.

If you would like to see Fatty Foulkes in action you can catch a glimpse of him in the Mitchell and Kenyon films playing for Sheffield United against Bury on September 6th 1902. You appreciate his stature when you see this lovely piece of English football history.

Foulke's League Champions medal 1899

United

Sheffield

Ernest (Nudger) **Needham**

Ernest Needham was born in the Whittington Moor area of Chesterfield in 1873 and by the time he was 16 years old was playing for Staveley, a team with a very good reputation. After some good showings with this club he moved on to Sheffield United, making his debut in 1891 in the Northern League, where they finished third. In that first season at United, young Ernest played in seven different positions and managed to score nine goals. In his second season he again played in seven different positions but this time only notched eight goals. He played, but did not score, in the record 10-0 away victory at Burslem Port Vale, an away win that United has never been bettered. At the end of this season, 1892-93, a test match between United and Accrington was played to see who would gain promotion to the first division of English football, United came away with a 1-0 victory. From the promotion game onwards, Needham more or less made the number 6 shirt his own for the next 11 seasons.

In the championship winning side of 1899, Ernest returned his best haul of goals in one season by finding the net on ten occasions. Five times his goals were the difference between drawing and winning games, and in the match against Blackburn Rovers, a noteable scalp in those days, he scored a hat-trick.

He was at the club when it became one of the founder members of the newly formed Football League Second Division in 1892 and within a year gained promotion to the top flight of English Football. Within 10 years, Needham would help Sheffield United become the best side in England. As well as helping United to the pinnacle of the English game he gained more England caps, 16, whilst a player for Sheffield United than any other player throughout the club's long history. He also captained the national side.

In Needham's heyday, around the end of the nineteenth and the beginning of the twentieth century, he was called the "Prince of Halfbacks". This was for good reason. He led Sheffield United to a League Championship in 1899 and two runners up placings in 1897 and 1900. Two FA Cup wins followed in 1899 and 1902. In between those two wins came a 1901 FA Cup defeat against a non league side, Tottenham Hotspurs. United were also one of the first two sides to play for what is now known as the Charity Shield in 1898 against the Corinthians. The Shield was shared after two drawn games.

United also, technically, won the British Championship when defeating Celtic, the Scottish Champions in a challenge match to decide who was the top football team in Britain.

Even the Manchester United, Chelsea and Arsenal sides of the present day would be more than pleased with those returns.

Ernest Needham played over 550 games for Sheffield United scoring 84 goals, which is an excellent return for a halfback. Nicknamed "Nudger", you would be allowed to think he did the odd push or shove, but he was never cautioned in his long career. With remarks from fellow internationals - "the greatest player association football has ever seen" - Needham really was a giant of those early footballing days, even though he only stood five foot six inches tall.

His stamina was legendary, making his way back to his own goal to help out with defensive duty and, literally, within seconds he was up with his forwards helping them score the goals that made Sheffield United one of the best sides of that era. It is said that if he had a flaw in his game, it was that he tried too hard to help out his players, he would try to do all the things he should, possibly, as the team captain, have been barking orders at his players to do.

People may have their differing opinions of who was their favourite Blades player, Hagan, Currie, Gillespie . . . but Ernest Needham must stand out as the all-time greatest footballer ever to pull on a Sheffield United shirt.

Ernest Needham's Football League v Ireland medal

United

Sheffield

Billy **Gillespie**

William Gillespie was born in Kerrykeel, Donegal on 6th August 1891 just around the time Sheffield United were finding their feet in the new football league. Nineteen years later, after playing for Derry Institue for a couple of seasons he made his way across the Irish Sea to sign for Leeds City. He stayed at Leeds for only one season, a prudent decision as Leeds City, some years later, were expelled from the league because of financial difficulties.

He moved to Bramall Lane in December 1911. The next twenty years were to see Billy score over 125 goals and play in over 550 games for Sheffield United. Within that period they won two FA Cup finals. Billy was to become one of Sheffield United's most famous and respected players in the years just before and after the First World War. In his first season, 1911-12, he scored 11 goals in 17 league appearances. That was enough for the fans to take Billy to their hearts and with his never say die attitude and his very respectable tally of goals he soon became a cult hero. In the fifteen seasons he played at the Lane he never failed to find the net, and in six, scored double figures.

He was also regularly selected for Ireland, when it was a united Ireland – football wise. On 25 occasions, he scored 13 times. Those 13 goals stood as the record for Northern Ireland, for 78 years, until David Healy struck his 14th international goal in the country's summer tour of the Caribbean. Gillespie had an absolutely incredibe scoring record against the English with seven of his 13 goals being scored against the old enemy. He started this stunning run by scoring both goals on his internationsl debut in 1913 in a 2-1 win over England. The next season, 1914, Ireland won the British Championship for the first time ever. They again beat England, Billy scoring agaiin, and Wales and managed a draw with Scotland at Windsor Park. This shows that Billy was playing in high class arenas at international and club level and was never found wanting. It was Billy who was becoming the star attraction. The 25 caps Gillespie won whilst playing for Sheffield United make him their most capped international. This would probably have been a much larger total but Billy sometimes decided to play for his club when selected for Ireland.

After gaining club and international acclaim the First World War came and not only devastated Europe for the next four years but also effectively ended English league football.

Sheffield United played longer than most in that last season before the War as they reached the 1915 FA Cup Final on April 24th when they beat Chelsea 3-0 at Old Trafford, Manchester. Unfortunately, Gillespie missed the match whilst suffering with a broken leg. I imagine Billy thought, even at the early age of 24, that with the outbreak of war it may have been his last chance to gain the most presitigious medal of them all, the FA Cup winners. The Cup final with Chelsea was also the only full FA Cup final ever played in wartime and was nicknamed the Khaki Cup Final.

Throughout the war years, Sheffield United carried on playing Regional Football but guest players and young local players made up the ranks and these games were more of a lottery.

Thankfully World War One came to an end in 1918 and full time league football resumed in Britain as well as across Europe. Through the war years, Gillespie only made about 50 appearances for the Blades as he was on active service.

Gillespie, now with a very receeding hairline, was still a fine player and settled into a more constructive midfield role from where he still notched his fair share of goals. He twice hit 14 goals in seasons 1921-22 and 1923-23 to show that he still had the touch.

After Billy suffered the broken leg and missed the Cup Final of 1915 he was was instrumental in the Blades lifting the trophy again 10 years later when they defeated Cardiff City 1-0 in the Wembley final.

In 1932, he left England and returned to Ireland for a nine-year stint as manager of Derry City. During his time as Brandywell boss, he not only changed the club's strip to their present day red and white stripes, but he also guided them to two City Cup triumphs as well as four successive Irish League runners-up spots and to the 1936 Irish Cup final where they lost 2-1 to Linfield at Celtic Park.

Billy Gillespie's English Cup Winners medal 1925, today's FA Cup

United

Sheffield

Harry **Johnson**

'Young Harry' was the son of 'old Harry' Johnson, the former international right half and another great Blades servant. 'Young Harry' was an ever-popular part-time professional with a vast amount of energy, enthusiasm and he was totally fearless when going in for that final touch in front of goal.

Born in the Ecclesfield area of Sheffield, he signed forms for the Blades during the First World War, in 1915. He played quite a few games for United during those war years, plus he also guested for Notts County, Birmingham City and Rotherham. After he was demobed from the Army in late 1919 he played throughout the next decade solely as the first choice number nine. And what a centre forward he was! Listed are his total goals per season from 1920 to 1930 respectively: 12, 13, 17, 19, 16, 21, 27, 24, 43, 31. In his record haul season 1927-28 he scored 33 league goals in 36 games and 10 FA cup goals in 8 games.

All of Young Harry's games were played in the top division, and in season 1925-1926 when United claimed their highest league position in Johnson's era, remarkably all five United forwards achieved double figure goal totals: Tunstall 20, Boyle 14, Gillespie 13, Menlove 12 and Johnson with 27.

Harry Johnson should probably have gained more representative caps than he did. One game for the English League, in which he scored a hat-trick, was his total haul of honours. How do you play one game, score three goals and get dropped?

Sheffield United's all time record goalscorer with over 250 goals to his name, Johnson was the club's leading scorer in nine out of his ten full seasons at Sheffield United and an FA Cup Final winner in 1925. In that cup run to Wembley, he scored five goals making him, once again, the clubs top FA cup scorer.

He scored five goals in one Boxing Day game against West Ham, scored four goals on seven occasions and 12 hat tricks. One of those hat tricks came against the old enemy, Sheffield Wednesday, in a FA Cup 5th round tie at Bramall Lane in 1928. The attendance for that game was just short of 60,000.

It is said that Harry would have scored more than double or treble his goal tally if he had taken all his chances, but surely that is the same with any forward past or present. Take Keith Edwards, as a more recent example of this problem. What it does prove is the instinct was there to get into those positions. Some of the present day strikers could do with a little of what Johnson had, Crouch, Saha, Beattie, etc have cost many millions of pounds for so little return.

Harry Johnson (Sheffield United)

Harry worked all week and looked forward to his game at the weekend. This is why Young Harry was so well loved, he was one of us. Just like the lads who played for the local pub or work teams, he did his bit during the week and tried his heart out on Saturday. Now a trier in Sheffield football is looked upon with respect, if a player is seen to be giving his all for his team that is as much as the crowd can ask. And just like any player, Harry, did have his lean spells, not that you would notice from his scoring statistics.

His father, also named Harry, and his younger brother Tom both played for United.

In 1931 Young Harry was transferred to Mansfield Town and far from it being an "out to pasture" move, Harry proceeded to knock in another 100 plus goals for the Stags and became their record leading scorer.

He retired in 1936 and passed away in Sheffield in May 1981.

A cigarette card of the day depicting Harry Johnson

United

Sheffield

Fred **Tunstall**

Freddy Tunstall played at outside left for Sheffield United 491 times in a career that spanned from 1920 until his £400 transfer to Halifax in 1933. He scored some memorable strikes in that 13 years span, with a total haul of 129 goals, but none more rewarding or famous than the only goal in the 1925 FA Cup Final against Cardiff City at Wembley Stadium in front of 91,763 fans. That was the last major trophy Sheffield United won. On the run to Wembley, which was only the third FA cup final played on the hallowed turf, United defeated the old enemy, Sheffield Wednesday, 3-2 in front of a 40,000 plus crowd at Bramall Lane.

Fred was born in Newcastle under Lyme in Staffordshire on 28th May 1897. The date of his birth given in some references is 29th March 1900 and his place of birth is given as Gravesend.

He moved along with his family to Darfield near Barnsley and gained work as a miner in Houghton Main Colliery. He was not a regular footballer as a young boy and it was not until he joined the army his football prowess came to the fore. Tunstall served in the Royal Horse Artillery from 1915 until his discharge in 1919, not a good era to be in the British Army. Tunstall came home and played in the local league for Darfield St George until he was spotted and signed by Scunthorpe United, who were a non league club at that time. Sheffield United and Barnsley had both looked at Fred but decided against signing him when he gave performances that did not impress. Quality scouting?

A couple of years later he did sign for Sheffield United from Scunthorpe in 1922 for £1,000, a record fee, for a non league club. And for the next decade or so he was an almost ever present, and along with Billy Gillespie created one of the best left sided pairings in English Football. All of Fred's career at Sheffield United was played in the top flight of English football.

Fred Tunstall was noted for his crossing ability and powerful shooting. This is verified by the prolific goalscoring pair of Harry Johnson and Jimmy Dunne, who both stated their record goals

tallies would not have been so high if they had not fed off many chances created when the opposing goalie had blocked or dropped one of Fred's ferocious shots.

Because of his powerful shooting he was elected as the club's penaly taker, a task he did with some aplomb and very rarely missed. However, on one occasion he did miss two in one game against Notts County, skying one over the bar and having the other saved.

Tunstall was also an England international who made seven appearances for his country between 1923 and 1925. He played against Scotland three times, Northern Ireland twice, Wales and France. In some reference it is said he was made captain for a match against Canada. The Canadian cap, if won, was probably gained on tour.

After an excellent career at United the much loved Fred Tunstall moved to Halifax in 1933. After a few games for Halifax Town he soon moved on, to Boston.

He became almost as big a cult figure at Boston as he was throughout his long career at Sheffield United. He became player manager after the Second World War and managed for two more spells. In between these two periods he was the trainer. His career with Boston lasted from 1936 until he retired as "trainer", aged 65 in 1962. Even this was not the end of Fred's love affair with Boston as he actually came out of retirement to manage the club for a season whilst they played in the Boston & District League in season 1964/5.

Fred Tunstall is Boston's longest serving manager – having been in charge for a total of almost 10 seasons over the years.

He was revered in Sheffield so much so that "fetch Tunstall" was still the cry in the early sixties if a home player missed a penalty.

Fred Tunstall passed away in 1971.

Fred Tunstall's Medal for the FA Tour of Canada

United

Sheffield

Jimmy **Dunne**

Born on September 3rd, 1905 in Dublin, Jimmy Dunne played Gaelic football as a child, and began his soccer career with the local team, Shamrock Rovers in 1923. It is rumoured that he honed his footballing skills in an internment camp during the Irish Civil War.

He moved to England in 1925 joining New Brighton, and quickly showing his mettle; scoring an impressive six times in eight Third Division North matches.

Jimmy was snapped up by Sheffield United as a shy, modest 20 year old. Unconvinced of his talent, and fearing that he would be outshone in the English First Division, he was initially reluctant to sign for the Blades, but was persuaded to join them in February 1926. He showed little of the enormous talent for which he would later become famous in the early seasons. In fact, he struggled to retain a first-team place!

In the 1929-30 season, however, Dunne became a goalscoring phenomenon. He was United's top scorer during four consecutive seasons, 1929-1933, and hammered home 41 league goals in 1930-31, a club record. His seasonal tally during those 4 seasons was well over the 40 goal average.

During this incredible season, Jimmy scored 41 league goals and a total of 50 in all games for United. This included five hat-tricks and one haul of four goals against Liverpool; his 41 goal tally remains the record in the top flight of the English League by an Irishman. He scored in both games against runaway league champions Arsenal in two 1-1 draws, he notched another goal in the 3-1 away victory over Sheffield Wednesday at

Jimmy Dunne (Sheffield United & Ireland)

Hillsborough, and scored all three against Manchester United as the reds tumbled to relegation.

He followed this by scoring in 12 consecutive games the following season.

As the Depression bit deep, Sheffield United found themselves in dire financial straits, and the sale of Dunne became inevitable. In September 1933, Jimmy was signed, as a replacement for Jack Lambert, by Arsenal for the then not insubstantial sum of £8,250. He made his debut against Middlesbrough on September 30, 1933 in a 6-0 win, and went on to score nine goals in 23 league games that season, collecting a well-deserved First Division winners' medal.

Dunne was ousted from the Arsenal first team with the arrival of Ted Drake, and would only play eight more games over the following two seasons.

Although Dunne was largely relegated to the reserves during his time at Highbury, his Arsenal teammates were more appreciative of his talents than the selectors. Cliff Bastin called him, "one of the best five centre forwards I have ever seen".

Dunne was eventually sold to Southampton in July 1936. He was the Saints' leading scorer in 1936-37, but returned to Shamrock Rovers in 1938.

After retiring as a player, Dunne became a coach at Rovers, and had a coaching spell at Bohemians between 1942 and 1947, before returning to his old club. He died suddenly, in his home town of Dublin, at the age of 44, in December 1949.

An outstanding player, Jimmy Dunne possessed many of the talents one would associate with truly great strikers: he had tremendous ball control, was an equally fine shot with both feet, had speed and was a phenomenal header of the ball.

Jimmy was an Irish international, winning 22 caps for his country and scoring 12 goals.

Over half a century after his tragically early death, Dunne still holds the record for most goals scored in a single season at the Lane.

A cigarette card of the day depicting Jimmy Dunne

United

Sheffield

Ephraim (Jock) **Dodds**

Ephraim Dodds was born in 1915 in Scotland and moved to County Durham when he was around 12 years old. It was obvious to his new friends that he was from across the border, so it was inevitable that his nickname would be Jock.

He was spotted by Huddersfield Town when only 16 years old, but did not make the grade there, nor at Lincoln City.

After the prolific goalscoring of young Harry Johnson and Jimmy Dunne over the previous fourteen years it was going to be difficult to find someone who could fill their place in the Sheffield United team. Unitedites had become used to a front player who regularly averaged around 30 goals per season.

So when Teddy Davison bought Ephraim (Jock) Dodds on a free transfer from Lincoln, no one thought this 18 year old who cost 'nowt' would be the one to take on the mantle of Sheffield United's top goalscorer.

It must be said that he would have a little easier life than those two great goalscorers as United had been relegated to Division Two just before Jock arrived.

And so on August 25, against Burnley at Bramall Lane, young Jock Dodds made his debut for United. It was a blank day for United and Dodds as the game was a 0-0 draw. He did score in his second match, a defeat against Oldham. During the next couple of months he was in and out of the side and was in fact dropped for a nine match period. When he regained his place in the side in late January he started to do the business. He notched 22 goals in 32 games in that first season. He scored 45 goals in 57 game in season 1935/36 as well as playing, albeit on the losing side, in the FA Cup Final at Wembley, where he nearly levelled the game when he rattled the crossbar with a fine header. He also has a prolific spell starting on Christmas Day 1935, against Swansea Town, where

he scored a hat-trick and proceeded to score two goals in each of his next four games.

Season 1936/37 showed another fine return of 28 goals in 44 appearances. In season 1937/38 he went one better, bagging 29 goals in 50 appearances. His fifth and final season for United still saw him reach 20 goals in just 34 games. He departed, after asking Teddy Davison for a transfer, in early March.

His statistics speak for themselves. He scored 113 league goals in 178 games and 10 goals in 17 FA Cup appearances. He also scored many other goals in friendlies - home and abroad - County Cup and benefit games.

Jock Dodds joined Blackpool when they were tottering on the brink of relegation, the Seasiders investing a, then, massive £10,000 on the player in March 1939.

He justified the faith placed in him and, with 10 goals in 12 games, helped keep First Division football at Bloomfield Road. He scored three times in three games to put Blackpool at the top of the First Division table in September 1939 just before Germany and World War II brought an official end to league football in Britain, for a 6 year duration.

Games played in wartime were more regionalised, but Jock still demonstrated his goalscoring skills to the full with 230 goals in only 157 games. Blackpool became the most successful side of the wartime era, winning three successive championships and beating Sheffield Wednesday in a two legged Cup Final in 1943. He also played at full international level for Scotland on one instance, scoring a hat-trick against the "auld" enemy.

Jock Dodds's 1936 FA Cup Runners Up Medal - A postcard showing a smiling Jock

United

Sheffield

Jimmy **Hagan**

Jimmy Hagan is to many supporters the best player to ever pull on the red and white striped shirt of Sheffield United. A player who could pass and shoot with both feet, had stunning ball control, was a regular goalscorer and had enough tricks in his locker to confound and astound any opposition player.

From an early age it was possible to see Hagan's potential. He became an international at schoolboy level. He was soon picked up by Liverpool at the age of just 14, but the football league regulation forbade such actions for one so young, and he returned home to County Durham. He was soon being chased by other clubs and Derby were the ones to get his signature. He made his Derby County debut in December 1935 just a few days short of his 18th birthday. His chances at Derby were limited as the club had a forward line of full internationals and Jimmy could not break through into the side.

So, at 20 years of age, in November 1938, he signed for Sheffield United. He immediately proceeded to orchestrate the United midfield and in his 28 league games scored ten goals.

In the last game of the season United needed a win to pip local rivals Sheffield Wednesday for promotion. Jimmy took the game against Spurs by the scruff of the neck and finished with a hat-trick of excellent goals, in a 6-1 home win, in front of a near 40,000 crowd. United won promotion and the crowd had a new hero.

The next season came and United started brightly, three wins and a draw. And then on the 3rd September 1939, Britain declared war on Germany and football was immediately suspended.

Sheffield United played throughout the war years in regional leagues and in the last of those war seasons were champions of the Football League North, a league that included Manchester United, Everton, Wednesday, Newcastle, Leeds.

Jimmy was demobbed in 1946 and was back in the side from mid September. He played 38 games and scored a very respectable 15 goals in a season when the Blades managed 6th position in the top division. This placing had not been bettered for over 20 years.

Hagan had gained 16 wartime England caps so the selectors gave him a chance against Denmark in 1948. Remarkably, this was Jimmy's only full appearance for the England side. He did gain other representative honours: Football League games, FA tour or Canada and Austrailia.

To show the extent of Hagan's worth in English football, city rivals, Sheffield Wednesday offered a British transfer record of £32,500 for his services. Thankfully, Hagan refused and stated he would like to finish his career at the Lane.

Besides a fantastic football peacetime career of over 440 games and scoring over 150 goals for United plus the few early league games for Derby County, he made over 100 wartime guest appeances for United, Aldershot and Huddersfield Town. Hagan had a football playing career that spanned over 22 years. Strangely enough his last game for the Blades in September 1957 was against his old club Derby County which United lost 0-2.

Jimmy then went into management with spells at Peterborough, West Bromwich Albion, Portugese sides Benfica and Sporting Libson.

At Peterborough he took them from non-league obscurity to runaway champions of Division 4. West Brom won the League Cup under his management and Benfica lifted three league titles in the early 1970s whilst he was in charge.

Sheffield United greatest player? Perhaps, but old Nudger Needham may run him close.

Jimmy Hagans' statue in Sheffield United's Hall of Fame and his Football League versus Ireland Medal

United

Sheffield

Joe **Shaw**

Joe Shaw was born in County Durham in 1928 and moved to the South Yorkshire area when still a young boy. He made his debut at the tender age of just 16 years of age in season 1944-1945 in the Football League North. This was the league that Sheffield United played in during the last few years of the Second World War. In fact Joe made two appearances that season, but he was deemed too ineffective in the inside forward position he was selected for. It was not until 1948-1949 season that Joe actually made his peacetime football league debut, starting three more games from the inside forward position. He was converted to the left wing half spot and from that point on Joe Shaw was to become synonymous with the Sheffield United back line until his last appearance 18 years later in Februrary 1966. Joe was the greatest servant Sheffield United Football Club has ever had, and in today's climate of money and self interest, it is unlikely that his haul of 690 football league and FA and League cup appearances will ever be beaten.

Shaw was an ever present in the side that gained promotion in season 1953 as Second Division Champions, playing in all 42 league games.

Within the next 18 months he had developed so much, manager Reg Freeman made him team captain. He was also selected for the 1955 England squad versus Scotland, albeit as official reserve. The sad fact is that Joe Shaw never gained a full England Cap. Now, every club has someone who was their best uncapped player in this or that position, but it must be said the England selectors were a little unfair to Shaw to never give him a chance in the full England side at centre half. Joe did gain representative honours when he played for the Football League a couple of times and went on the English Football Association tour of Austrailia.

In season 1955/56 a new manager arrived at the Lane, Joe Mercer. Now, the new boss did not think too highly of having a

centre half who was only 5 foot 8 inches tall at the centre of his back line. It took the best part of two seasons for Shaw to prove to Mercer that wearing the number five shirt was indeed in his and the club's best interests. To be fair to Mercer, it was he who put together the defence of Hodgkinson, Coldwell, G Shaw, Richardson, J Shaw and Summers. Out of the six players only Summers, who cost a fee of £3,000 from WBA, did not to come through the ranks at United. This solid group of defender had very few injuries and played as a unit for almost six years. It was only when Bernard Shaw ousted his brother Graham and Len Badger displaced Cec Coldwell that the defence took on an unfamiliar look. In 1961, during that spell of the unchanging defence, United won promotion back to the top division and played in the FA Cup semi-final against Leicester, where after two goalless games, United lost 2-0 in the third. Unfortunately, Graham Shaw missed a penalty for United. Whether United would have been strong enough to beat Spurs in the Cup Final and stop them doing the double for the first time in the 20th century is anybody's guess. But a cup final appearance for that side would have been some reward for the joy they gave the fans around Bramall Lane at that period.

Joe still kept plodding on in that centre half position keeping all the young reserve centre halves where they belonged in the Central League side and keeping all the centre forwards of the day where they belonged, in his pocket.

After his retirement, Joe coached young players at Sheffield United for 18 months and then moved into management, first with York City and then Chesterfield until 1976.

> JOE SHAW TESTIMONIAL FUND
> Sheffield United v Selected XI
> Monday, 29th March, 1965
> Kick-off 7.30 p.m.
> ROW SEAT
> H | 177
> CENTRE STAND
> BENEFIT MATCH RESERVED SEAT 10/-

Joe Shaw's boots - A ticket stub for his testimonial match - both of which are on display in the Hall of Fame

Sheffield

Alf **Ringstead**

Alfred Ringstead was born on 14th October, 1927 in Dublin, but he only spent his first two years on the Emerald Isle, moving to Wales in 1929. Ringstead's father was a jockey of some repute but young Alf was not to follow in his fathers footsteps, instead he plumped for football as his sport of choice. At the tender age of 14 he was being watched by Everton and Bolton Wanderers but did not feel too happy with either club and decided instead to play for his local side, Ellesmere Port.

Whilst playing part time for Ellesmere he worked as an upholsterer before joining the army, serving some time in India. After his national service he joined Northwich Victoria in the Cheshire League and only played a handful of games before Sheffield United scouts noticed his goalscoring displays and quickly persuaded manager Teddy Davision to sign him in November 1950. Ringstead was 23 years old at the time and his transfer fee was £2,500.

At the beginning of December 1950 he made his United debut against Coventry City at Bramall Lane in front of a near 30,000 crowd. Ringstead immediately became a favourite with a well taken header and an excellent debut display in a 2-0 win. He also scored in his next two matches, both away games at Manchester City and Blackburn respectively. He played 24 league games and scored 10 goals in his first season, 1950-1951.

His next season was very special indeed, he scored 27 league and FA Cup goals and gained full international recognition with Ireland. To Blade fans he achieved God like status with two goals in a 7-3 drubbing of Sheffield Wednesday at Bramall Lane in front of over 51,000 supporters. Three months later, at Hillsborough, in front of the record Sheffield derby crowd, 63,327, he again bagged a brace of goals, when

United, once again, won 3-1. He finished club top scorer in his first full season. His four colleagues along the United forward line also all reached double figures: Brook 17, Hawksworth 12, Smith 11 and Hagan 10,

After a season like 1951-52 it would be very hard for Alf to carry on in this vein, but amazingly, he did. In season 1952-53 he was ever present playing all 42 league games and once again scoring over 20 goals. And, again, the other forwards weighed in with more than their fair share of goals: Browning 18, Hagan 18, Brook 17 and Hawksworth 10. All this culminated in Sheffield United winning promotion as Second Division Champions.

After promotion, when games were obviously harder, Ringstead still managed to score into double figures and finish club top scorer, this in a season where relegation was only missed by one place.

Season 1954-55 was a little better when the Blades managed 13th place and manager Freeman played Ringstead in 30 games where he returned 11 goals. Unfortunately, the United manager suffered a short illness and died during the close season and Joe Mercer was recruited. Now whilst Mercer can be credited with sorting out the defence over the long term, it must be said he did tinker with the side early on. He played 28 players in his first season in charge: trying three keepers, six centre forwards and even had the temerity to drop Jimmy Hagan, only right full back Cec Coldwell was an ever present with 42 league games. Relegation in bottom spot followed.

Ringstead was never used on a regular basis again, playing 7, 20 and 16 games in the next three seasons respectively. As if to sign off on a high note, Ringstead scored a hat-trick of headers in one of his last games for United against Scunthorpe.

He was sold by Joe Mercer to Mansfield in 1959.

One of Alf Ringstead's Irish Caps versus Norway, a game in which he scored in a 3-1 victory - A cigarette card showing Alf in caricature

United

S h e f f i e l d

Graham **Shaw**

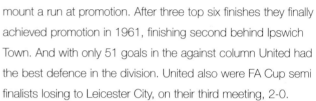

Graham Shaw was 17 years old when he made his debut for Sheffield United in the intense derby atmosphere of Hillsborough. Over 65,000, mostly hostile, fans were expecting the Owls to overturn the debacle of the season's previous derby, at Bramall Lane, when United won 7-3 . The Owls fans saw the possibility of a weak link when they heard that a young untried player would be in the United defence. Shaw did not let his teammates down that January afternoon, when the Blades won 3-1. Throughout the other 497 games he played for the Blades, he was equally as dependable

Graham was born in Sheffield in 1934 and went to Southey Green School, where the family home was situated nearby on Parson Cross. Young Shaw was good at most sports but excelled at football, boxing and cricket. In fact, at boxing, he was an ABA junior champion.

United spotted his footballing potential and requested he turn out for Oaks Fold, a Shiregreen based club, which was a nursery club for the Blades. He produced some fine displays and merited a call up to the reserves. It was at this stage that United offered the youngster a contract and requested he drop his interest in boxing.

After that derby day debut in January 1952, Graham only played two more games that season.

The following season was a different story with Shaw gaining and keeping his place in the back line for 37 of the possible 42 league games. He also scored two league goals in a game at Southampton when the Blades managed a creditable 4-4 draw. From that point on until the end of United's promotion winning season they only lost one game, the very last one, against Hull City.

Graham was now a regular in the first team line up and managed well over 50 games in his next two seasons. The following two seasons saw Graham serve his national service in the Army's Royal Signals regiment. Unfortunately, during that period, the Blades were relegated.

Graham slotted back into the left back spot and United proceeded to mount a run at promotion. After three top six finishes they finally achieved promotion in 1961, finishing second behind Ipswich Town. And with only 51 goals in the against column United had the best defence in the division. United also were FA Cup semi finalists losing to Leicester City, on their third meeting, 2-0.

The season that followed was a joy to behold: a double over Sheffield Wednesday, two fine draws with the double winning side Spurs, an away win at Manchester United, a home victory over the league runners up and cup finalists Burnley and another home win over Ipswich Town, the eventual winners of the top division in 1962.

The Blades 5th place in the top flight is a feat not bettered since and you have to go back to 1907 to see Sheffield United in a higher league placing when they finished 4th.

Shaw was selected to play for England on five occasions between 1958 and 1962. He never appeared on a losing side, winning three: Soviet Union 5-0, Scotland 1-0, Wales 4-0 and drawing two: Italy 2-2, Wales 2-2.

The rest of Graham Shaw's Sheffield United career was played out in the top division. His last appearance came in a 4-3 home victory over West Bromwich Albion in October 1966, nearly 15 years after his home debut against the Owls.

Graham moved to Doncaster Rovers and had a brief foray into non league player management with Scarborough, which lasted for a year.

Graham was the owner of a couple of snack bars in the old Sheffield Market where he could be found immaculately dressed in his white overall overseeing his staff and chatting to the customers. He also ran the Sportman Inn pub on Denby Street very close to his beloved Bramall Lane.

Graham's younger brother, Bernard, also made over 150 appearancees for the Blades.

Graham's Second Division Championship medal, which can be seen in Sheffield United Hall of Fame - Graham's England Blazer

S h e f f i e l d

Derek (Doc) **Pace**

Derek Pace was born in 1932 in Essington and signed for Aston Villa, when just 17, from Bloxwich Scouts in September 1949. Almost immediately Derek was called up to do his two years' National Service in the Medical Corps from where he obtained the nicknamed "Doc". His opportunities were limited at Aston Villa, even though he scored on his debut against Burnley on the 17th March 1951.

Derek Pace was one of a number of centre forwards tried by Aston Villa following the departure of Trevor Ford to Sunderland. He played in six league games and scored six goals, a record you may think deserved slightly more of a run in the first team. Over the next few seasons, Derek struggled to gain a regular place in the first team at Villa. Things did pick up in season 1956-7 with Pace playing in 21 league matches, scoring six league goals, and in his six FA cup games he notched two more goals. He must have been devastated to learn he was 12th man and not in the cup final side of 1957, especially after playing in the six cup matches previously.

The following season, 1957-58, he played in the Charity Shield side that lost to Manchester United and played in 12 league games scoring three goals. It was at this stage, December 1957, that Sheffield United moved in and signed Pace. He had scored 42 league and cup goals in 106 matches at Villa.

Pace made his debut for Sheffield United on Boxing Day December 1957, in front of 25,500 Blades supporters. He had just been signed from Aston Villa for a reasonable sum of £12,000 and the crowd turned up to see whether Joe Mercer had made a sound buy. They had just eight minutes to wait before "Doc" notched the first of many goals he would go on to score for United.

Derek was small in stature, for a centre forward, but tenacious, deceptively quick and always willing to go in where it hurt to get the last touch for that goalscoring opportunity.

Pace was a real opportunist centre forward, scoring 140 goals in 253-league appearance, (175 goals in 302 league and cup games).

Derek started his first campaign, 1957-58, with 22 games and a return of 16 goals. in the next six season's Derek posted goal figures of 29, 28, 26 in Blades promotion year, 25, 19 and 15 goals in 1963-64, his final full season.

He was United's top scorer for all his seven seasons at Bramall Lane before moving on to Notts County in December 1964. He played 29 matches and scored 15 goals. He then moved on to Walsall in July 1966, only playing four matches plus one as substitute. He scored one goal, a flying header at Grimsby, in August 1966, just over 15 years after his first ever league goal for Aston Villa.

Derek scored goals against many sides but he seemed to up his ratio against his old club, Aston Villa, with seven goals in eight games. One game at Villa Park saw Pace score a hat-trick, in a 3-1 win, how he must have loved that. He also liked to pop a few in against Sheffield Wednesday with six strikes in eight games.

In his career he scored a grand total of 233 goals in 444 games an average of one goal every 1.9 matches. You don't get many strikers in today's game who can offer up a goalscoring return of this quality or ratio.

After retiring from professional football Derek Pace became a sales representative for Churchfield Springs Ltd of West Bromwich

He died, following a heart attack, at the early age of 57 on the 17th October 1989.

Programme Sheffield United v Sheffield Wednesday. FA Cup sixth round. Crowd 59,692

U n i t e d

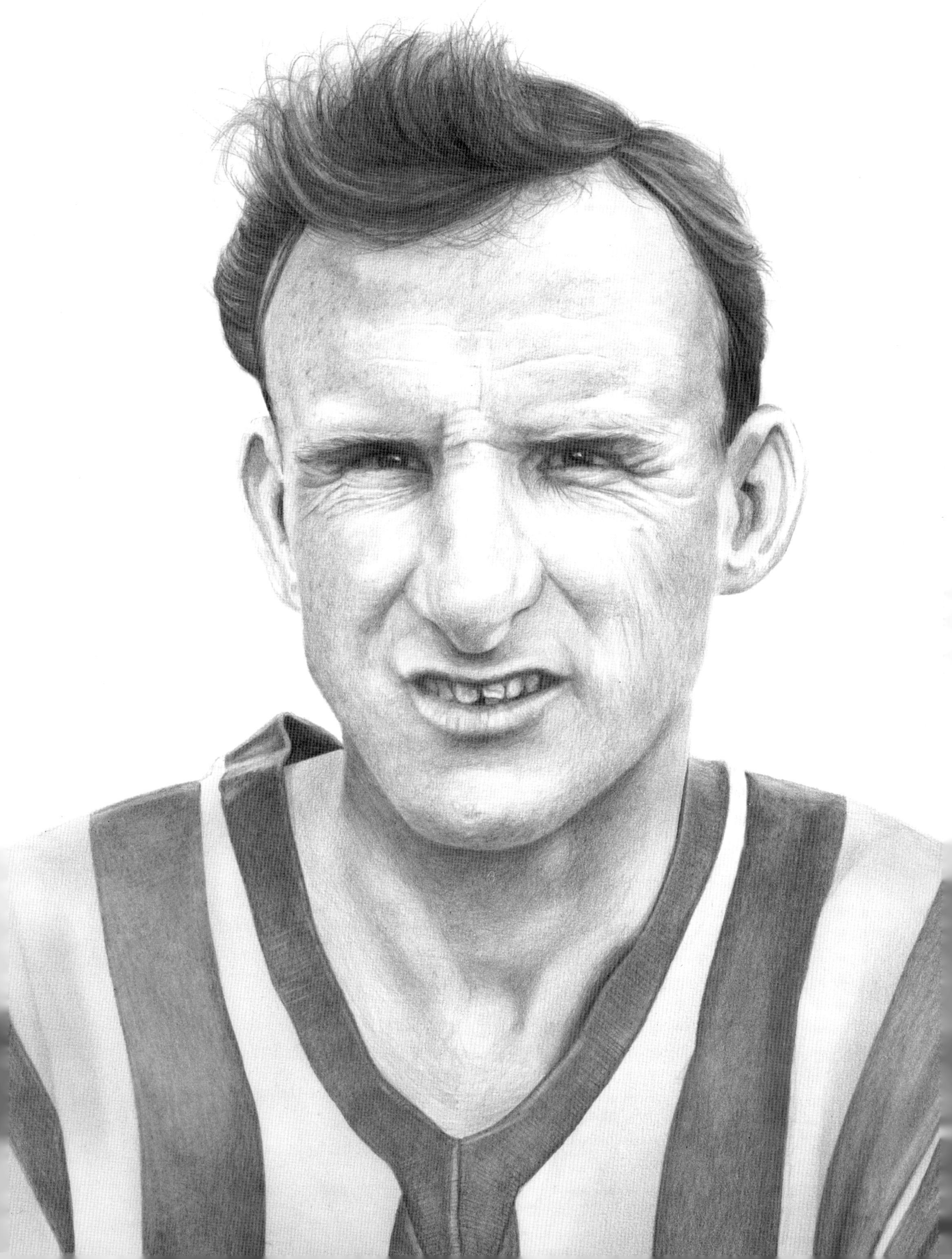

Sheffield

Cec **Coldwell**

Cec Coldwell played 410 league games and 41 cup games, putting him in the top ten player list of all time appearances for Sheffield United.

Cec was born in January 1929 in Dungworth, a small village near Stannington, on the western outskirts of Sheffield. When old enough he played football for the local works team. Coldwell was spotted and given a trial with Bradford City and he was signed by the club. However, Cec, did not fancy the club and so returned home and started to play for Norton Woodseats. It was playing for the South Sheffield side that he was spotted by the Sheffield United scouts and he duly signed professional forms in late 1951. Six months later in April 1952 he was given his first team debut against Southampton in a 1-0 home win. Coldwell only played friendly games the following season and it was not until an October 1953 County Cup Final against local rivals Rotherham that he appeared again in the first team. It was a resounding 5-0 thumping of United's neighbours and was the real beginning of Coldwell's first team career.

Coldwell was not put straight into the side without a fight from the chap he was trying to replace, Fred Furniss, a player who himself made over 300 league and cup appearances for the Blades. Furniss bounced back a couple of times to reclaim his left back spot, but Coldwell's consistency and the ageing of Furniss made the replacement inevitable.

Coldwell must have been grateful for the managerial takeover of Joe Mercer, even though it was in tragic circumstances, the previous manager Reg Freemen dying after a short illness. Mercer was a man who liked to keep a settled defence and when he finally decided on Joe Shaw playing at centre half, and a season or so later purchased Gerry

Summers from West Bromwich Albion, the defensive jigsaw was in place.

The defence of Hodgkinson, Coldwell, Graham Shaw, Richardson, Joe Shaw and Summers would be the sound base of a side which was probably the best since the 1925 cup final team. These six players made well over 2600 first team appearances for Sheffield United.

Joe Mercer eventually made Coldwell captain and therefore started a chain of events that over the next three decades would see Cec take up nearly every position at the club from youth, reserve and first team player, club captain, coach, first team coach and then acting manager, the last position on two separate occasions, in 1975 and again in 1977.

It is testament to Cec Coldwell that in all the positions he filled at Sheffield United Football Club he was never lacking and did every one of the jobs with the same committment and gusto which he showed upon his arrival at the club, as a 21 year old, in 1951.

People who remember Coldwell will recall his no frill attitude to defending. This was in stark contrast, at times, to his full back teammate Graham Shaw. Shaw was a more cultured ball player who the crowd loved, but he was caught in possession of the ball on many more occasions than the more industrious and straightforward Coldwell.

Coldwell made over 460 appearances for United but he only ever found the net on two occasions. Swansea Town in November 1959 were the unlucky side who he scored his first goal against in a 3-3 draw at Bramall Lane. His second goal came in the promotion winning season of 1961 against Leyton Orient in a 4-1 home victory.

Cec Coldwell's testimonial programme versus an All Star XI

Sheffield

Alan **Hodgkinson**

What can you say about Alan Hodgkinson. He was the best goalkeeper Sheffield United have ever had.

This is a bold statement when you think of the keepers the Blades have had: Bill Foulke – England International, Harold Gough – England International, Jim Brown – Scottish International, Alan Kelly – Eire International, Ted Burgin, Simon Tracey, Jack Smith – all high class custodians. The excellent, Paddy Kenny's long term standing cannot be assessed, just yet.

Alan was the complete goalkeeper: he was fast off his line, an amazingly agile shotstopper, brave to the point of recklessness and had a positional awareness I have only seen bettered by Gordon Banks.

Hodgkinson, along with Ron Springett of Sheffield Wednesday and Eddie Hopkinson of Bolton, shared the England international jersey for around seven years from 1956 until 1963. Hodgy and Springett were the two keepers who went to the 1962 World Cup finals in Chile. All three keepers were small in stature but were very rarely beaten by international opposition forwards.

Sheffielder Gordon Banks took over the mantle of England keeper in 1964 but his career was cut short by a road accident in the early 70s. From that point onwards it always seemed the giant, top heavy keepers, Shilton, Woods, James, Seaman, Robinson have been selected. They shouldn't even be allowed to utter Woods' or James' names in the same breath as Hodgkinson.

Alan started his league career with a 2-1 away win at Newcastle United in 1954 in front of a crowd of over 52,000 baying Geordie fans – some debut. He vied with Ted Burgin for nearly three full seasons before finally seeing him off in 1957. Burgin was well liked by the Bramall Lane crowd and had been in the first team since 1949, amassing well over 250 league appearances, but Hodgkinson's form merited his first team selection.

Alan's first three full seasons for United were in Division Two (now the Championship) where they were placed 6th, 3rd and 4th respectively before clinching promotion in 1961 when finishing second in the league.

The next season, 1961-62, Sheffield United finished 5th in the top division a feat they have not bettered since. In fact the last time United finished higher than fifth was 98 years ago, in 1907. It was a glorious season, with a double over the old enemy Sheffield Wednesday. Pace scored all three goals and Hodgy only conceded one - this in front of almost 90,000 people for both games. At Old Trafford Pace scored in a 1-0 win. Two creditable draws with the double winning side Spurs, and wins against Arsenal and Wolves, home and away. United also reached the 6th round of the FA cup.

The following season, 1962-63, Alan only missed two league games and in the 20 games he played at Bramall Lane only conceded 17 goals.

For the next four seasons, United were settled in mid table until the 1967-68 season when relegation reared its ugly head once again.

Alan, was, at this stage, playing the best football of his career and in season 1969-70 when finishing 6th in the second division he only conceded 38 goals in 41 league matches. In his 20 games at the Lane, he only had 10 goals in the against column. The very next season, Hodgkinson played the first 24 games. The 24th and last game of his Sheffield United career was away against Bolton Wanderers and sadly ended in a 2-1 defeat. He would have the benefit though of seeing his beloved United gain promotion.

After starting his career in a team that included the likes of Jimmy Hagan, Alf Ringstead, Fred Furniss, Joe Shaw, Graham Shaw and Tommy Hoyland, he finished in a side that also had a few United heroes: Woodward, Currie, Badger, Dearden, Hemsley, Reece, Colquhoun and Tudor.

Hodgkinson, Coldwell, Shaw G, Richardson, Shaw J and Summers were synonymous with Sheffield United's resolute defending, between them playing well over 2500 league games for the club as well as 241 FA cup games.

Alan Hodgkinson's England Cap for the game against Wales - Season 1960-1961

United

Sheffield

Len **Badger**

Len Badger played for England Schoolboys whilst at Coleridge Road School in Attercliffe, and was always destined to be a top class sportsman. He excelled at most sports but it was at football that he made his name in Sheffield. He progressed through the ranks at schoolboy level: Sheffield, Yorkshire and into the Engand side. A picture of Len Badger, in his England shirt, adorned the wall of Coleridge Road School assembly hall for many a year.

Len Badger also went on to be capped at Youth and Under 23 level but never received full international honours. It must be said there were some players gaining caps for the right back position who weren't in the same class as the young Sheffielder.

Len Badger probably had the most unenviable job in English football. To make a name for himself at Sheffield United he had to break into THE DEFENCE that had served the Blades for many years. He replaced Cec Coldwell, a united institution, and then even had the temerity to go on and make more first team appearances than Cec. Len made 510 appearances in league, FA cup and League cup games. Len has only been bettered by a few United greats - Joe Shaw 690, Alan Hodgkinson 652, Alan Woodward 591 and Ernest Needham 513. Needham's total is only league and FA cup appearances.

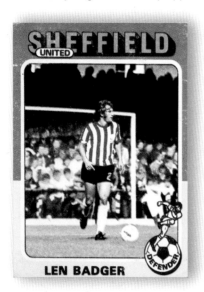

Forcing his way past the old war horse, Cec Coldwell was never going to be easy. So it proved with the older player showing his skill and making the highly rated Badger sit in the reserves. In fact it took three full season with Len only getting the odd game here and there. He played no league games in his first season, just friendly appearances. His second season was slightly better with one league game and one league cup game. His third season was a little bit of a breakthrough with seven league games and one appearance in each of the cups. By the start of season 64-65, Coldwell was heading for his 36 birthday and

the manager placed Badger in the starting line-up. From this point onwards the right back spot was to become as synonymous with the name of Badger as it had been with Coldwell for the previous 13 seasons.

Len Badger came up against the best players in British football. He played against the likes of George Best, John Connelly, Alan Ball, Terry Paine, Colin Dobson, John Sissons, and Derek Temple, all of them capped at some level. He was never found wanting with his speed and ability to read what the opponent's next move might be.

Some of his performances in the mid to late sixties warranted England selection. He did seem the complete full back. It has been written that he lacked a powerful physique, a statement that seems at odds with his tigerish tackles and remarkable ability to cover a team mate's errors. For a few years he seemed to be from the same mould as Joe Shaw, a player who seemed to cover for all the other members of the defence. Possibly the real reason he never achieved full international status was more to do with the club he played for.

Badger's long career as a Sheffield United first team player started in 1962 and lasted over 13 years until his final game, which was played at Bramall Lane, against Manchester United on December 13th, 1975. Unfortunately, it turned out to be a disastrous season for the Blades, ending in relegation with only 22 points gained for the whole season, only five of them gained at the halfway stage. This was a gigantic disapointment after season 1974-75 when they had finished 6th in the top flight of English football.

At the latter stages of his career, Len was transferred to Chesterfield where he played until hanging his boots up. He delved into the licencing trade, a career he stayed in for a quite a few years.

Len Badger was given a testimonial match by Sheffield United in 1974 when the Blades played Sheffield Wednesday in a 1-1 draw in front of over 23,000 appreciative fans.

Badger was a player whose team mates and fans, alike, instantly warmed to. I think they saw that Len's commitment was always 100% red and white effort.

A remarkable servant to the Blades.

A 1974 Topps Bazooka card, number 19, depicting Sheffield United's Len Badger

United

Sheffield

Mick **Jones**

Mick Jones was only in Sheffield United's first team for about four years, but he is still fondly remembered by Blades fans.

A big strong bustling lad, he made his debut against Manchester United in 1963 and kept his place to play against the other Mancunian side, City, four days later. This match was played at Maine Road on 24th April, which just happened to be Mick's 18th birthday. Jones duly celebrated by notching two goals in a 3-1 away win, the other goal coming from his strike partner Derek Doc Pace.

The Doc was nearing the end of his United career, but he still had a few tricks up his sleeve and enough experience and advice to hand out to help young Jones secure himself in the first team. They played as a strike partnership in six of the last seven games in season 1962-1963 and between them scored seven goals.

The following season, 1963-1964, saw United finish in mid table position and young Jones consolidate his position in the team, making 26 league and FA Cup appearances, scoring eight goals. Derek Pace, even in his last full season, was still showing the youngster the ropes in top flight football and as if to prove who was the main striker notched 15 goals in 31 appearances.

By the end of August the following season, Pace was sold and manager John Harris thought Mick Jones was now the finished article and able to lead the line without the experience of an older head. A new youngster had appeared on the scene, Alan Birchenall, and Harris deemed this would be his front two. Harris also had another young lad coming along nicely, Alan Woodward, so the front line was looking very bright for the future.

Jones produced his best figures yet with 14 league and three FA Cup goals from 42 games. With, the youngsters,

Birchenall and Woodward weighing in with another 20 between them the goal scoring mantle looked as though it might be spread out more evenly. For the last six or seven years it did seem as though the main goal scoring role had been carried by one man, Pace.

Season 1965-66 was an excellent season for Mick, himself, now the established United forward, scoring 21 goals in 40 games. This was more the ratio that the fans were looking for, and what the England selectors were looking for, Mick gained two full England caps in 1965. Unfortunately the other United forwards had gone off the boil and a measly eight goals from Birchenall put him as second top goalscorer.

Jones's last full season saw him keep up this high ratio with 18 League and FA Cup goals from 37 games. The Blades finished in the top half of the First Division of English Football and looked to be a side with real potential. United, at this time, had on their books, youngsters like: Mick Jones, Alan Birchenall, Alan Woodward, Len Badger, Gil Reece, Bernard Shaw, Geoff Salmons. It really did look as though the future was bright.

So it came as a real shock in season 1967-68 when, in September, United sold Jones to Leeds United. This was bad enough, but then Birchenall was sold to Chelsea. To cap a terrible year, relegation came to call at the end of the season.

Mick Jones, went on to win more England honours with Leeds, and on the domestic front won the Championship in 1974 and a FA Cup winners' medal in 1972.

A fine young player who was allowed to leave when a stronger club decision may have produced a totally different history for Sheffield United FC.

Programme: Sheffield United v Manchester United, Boxing Day 1966, Mick Jones & Alan Birchenall both scored in a 2-1 win

U n i t e d

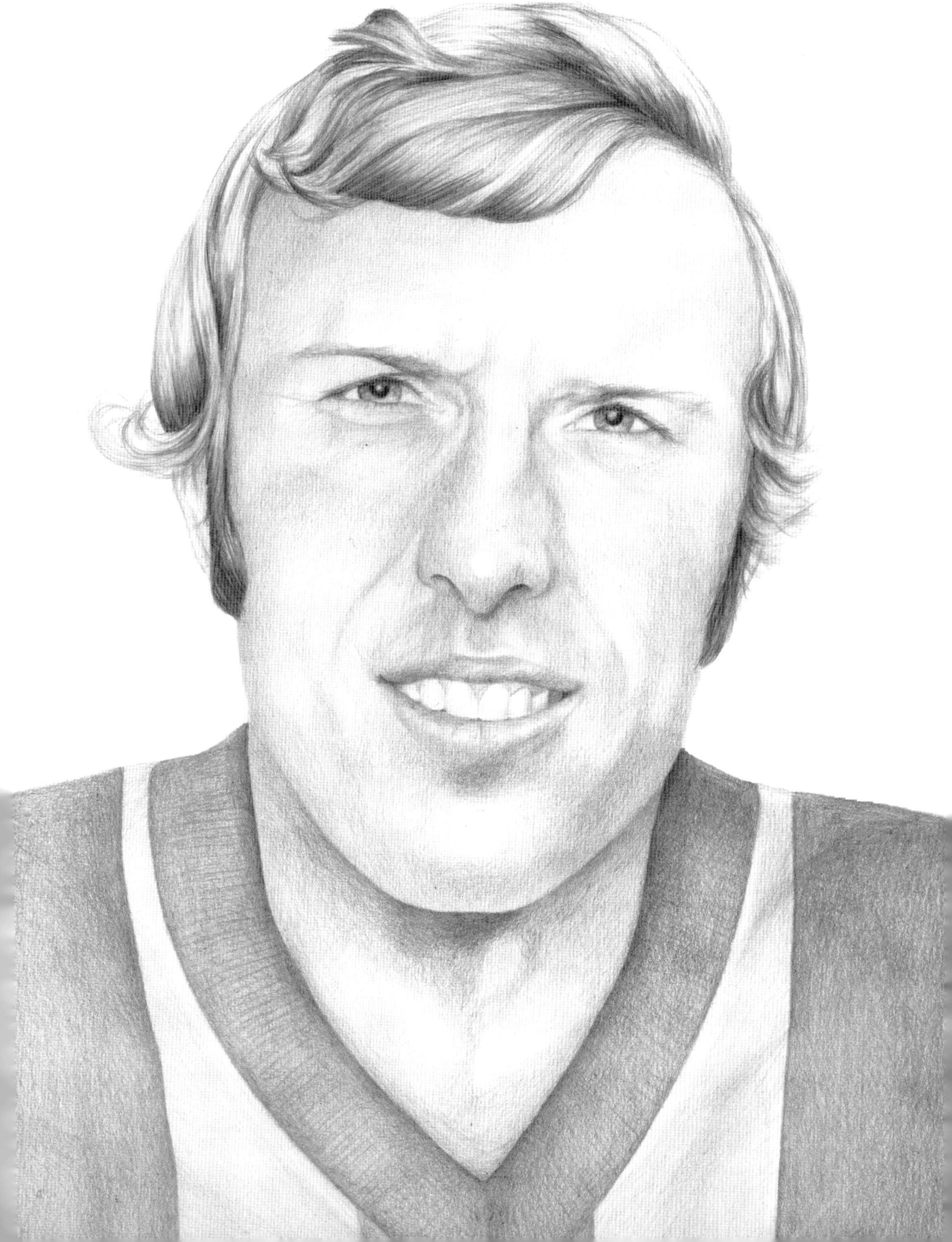

Sheffield

Alan **Woodward**

Alan Woodward's progress was probably being monitored by quite a few clubs as a young teenager who played for Barnsley Boys when they won the English Schools Shield. He signed apprentice forms a year later for local side Sheffield United at the tender age of 15.

Alan made his full Sheffield United, First Division debut, just after his 18th birthday, on October 1964 against Liverpool at Anfield. An unauspicious start as the Blades lost 4-1.

He had a season or so settling into the United first team but, soon after his debut he was able to hold onto his right wing position in the side.

For the following 14 seasons, Alan would supply the United front runners with accurate crosses and marvellous corner kicks. He also weighed in with 175 league and cup goals.

Woodward came into the United side whilst they were a top flight, Division One, club and to be honest he never really scored that many goals in those first 125 league appearances. In fact he only notched 27 league goals.

After relegation to the second division, in season 1967-68, United spent three season before gaining a second spot in the league and promotion. Woodward was top scorer at the Lane in all those three seasons, and this from a right wing position.

Back in Division One in 1971-72, he carried on as though the rise in class did not matter. He scored against Everton and Leicester away, in both games scoring the only goal. He scored against Arsenal, Fulham, Coventry (both games), Forest, Manchester City, Huddersfield, Southampton, Stoke, Wolves, Leicester again and hit four against Ipswich Town. He could not quite match his record of the last three seasons, though, because Billy Derden pipped him by one goal as leading scorer. Dearden scored 16 and Alan Woodward 15 goals.

The following season was not as good for the team or Alan but United still had some good results. Against Manchester United, they won 1-0 with Woodward scoring the only goal. Victories over Arsenal, Tottenham, Chelsea, a good away win at Manchester United to complete the double, West Brom, Birmingham and Crystal Palace. Woodward finished with 11 league and cup goal.

Woody got back on the goal trail the next season when United finished 6th in Division One, a position not bettered since. He scored 13 goals and played in all 42 league games. It was a very tight finish at the top with only four points separating the top six sides. United lost a home evening game against Derby County, who were the eventual champions. A win for United that night would have meant the Blades would have finished with 51 points along with Derby and Liverpool.

Amazingly, the very next season, United finished bottom of the league with just 22 points and only 52 goals scored. Alan notched 10 of those 52, making him United's top scorer. The next two full seasons saw him reach double figures in goals and play regularly, but his final season was to be a very sad one all around with only five games played and to cap it all United sank to Division three.

Alan Woodward's appearance in 595 league and cup matches is only beaten by Joe Shaw and Alan Hodgkinson and his goalscoring feats of 175 league and cup goals only bettered by young Harry Johnson. John Harris once said of Woodward "He simply has no conception of how much talent he has".

Alan was honoured at Youth and Football League level but, sadly, never managed a full England cap.

Alan joined Tulsa Roughnecks in the USA soccer league and played there for three seasons. He also played American Grid-Iron football as a kicker for one season turning out for Oklahoma Thunder. He still resides in Tulsa.

A 1974 Topps Bazooka card, number 205, depicting Sheffield United's Alan Woodward

Sheffield

Eddie **Colquhoun**

After relegation from Division One in 1968, United changed their manager, moving John Harris upstairs to General Manager and making Arthur Rowley the new man in charge. Unfortunately, Rowley was not a well liked man in his one year in charge at Bramall Lane. Within a short space of time he had sold off several well liked players: Carlin, Mallender, the Wagstaff brothers, Munks and Bernard Shaw. He brought in new personal who he thought could do the job he demanded: John Tudor, Ted Hemsley, David Powell, John Flynn and paid £27,500 for Eddie Colquhoun from West Brom. He made 23 year old Colquhoun his new team captain. But the results expected and instant return to Division One was not achieved. He was sacked. In retrospect it seems he was a manager of some insight. Almost all his buys became firm favourites at the Lane and, to be fair, none of the departing players were successes after leaving United. But football doesn't work like that, and after he was sacked, back came John Harris to steer the ship.

Eddie Colquhoun was born in Prestonpans, East Lothian in 1945 and was spotted 17 years later playing local football by Bury's Scottish scout, Jimmy Finnigan. He signed full professional terms around his 18th birthday and that same year, 1963 was selected to play for the Scotish side in the European Youth Tournament.

EDDIE COLQUHOUN

Eddie's boss at Bury was Bob Stokoe, the ex Newcastle United stalwart who later became Sunderland manager when they won the FA Cup in 1973. It was Stokoe who moulded Colquhoun into the central defender so reliable for Sheffield United and Scotland.

Ex Lane hero Jimmy Hagan spotted young Eddie's potential and signed him for WBA in early 1967 for a nominal fee. He was injured just before the Cup Final win against Everton and did not play at Wembley. What is a little surprising is that Colquhoun was allowed to leave for Sheffield United in October 1968.

The Rowley decision to make Eddie captain was never questioned and he gave Sheffield United a powerful figure who led by example and helped the younger defenders around him to develop.

He was also one of those centre halves who have this knack of helping out at set pieces and Colquhoun scored 21 league goals for the Blades in his 363 games. With Alan Woodward swinging in the corners or free kicks at just the height Eddie liked, he made the opposition defences and goalkeepers work hard to prevent him scoring, which on many occasions they couldn't.

Eddie was a big man and coming up against some of the tougher centre forwards of the day the scene was often set for some bruising encounters. Richie, Lockhead, MacDonald, O'Hare, Hickton, ex Blade Jones and Clarke gave and asked for no quarter.

Under Colquhoun's leadership in 1971, Sheffield United gained promotion back to the top flight, with the big man scoring six goals. Three of those goals dictating that United won the game instead of only gaining a draw. It was during that season back in Division One and up against the top class of British football that Eddie started to shine even brighter. It was not long before the Scottish national team came knocking at the door, giving him the first of his nine full caps for his country.

Ken Furphy, now in contol of United in season 1973-74 relieved Eddie of the captaincy and gave it to Tony Currie. This seemed to be a reasonable decision as the following season was United best for many years. But within 12 months United were relegated and Currie had gone to Leeds United. Eddie was never given the captain's arm band back and the leadership qualities he showed were never again used to the full. Before the ingnominy of United's relegation to division three, Eddie left for US soccer, Detroit Express, then moving to be player coach at Washington Diplomats, also in the US League.

A 1974 Topps Bazooka card, number 46, depicting Sheffield United's Eddie Colquhoun

United

Sheffield

Trevor **Hockey**

Trevor Hockey was a footballing wanderer. He had a professional career that spanned 16 years, including seven clubs and almost 600 first team appearances.

Hockey only played 78 games for Sheffield United, scoring four goals along the way. He played in the last 17 games of the promotion season and was only on the losing side twice. His next two seasons were to see him play 28 and 23 games respectively when United finished mid table.

Hockey was a Yorkshireman by birth, being born in Keighley on 1st May 1943. As a schoolboy, Trevor played Rugby League, Rugby Union and Football, but in the end he chose to try and make soccer his full time career.

He was watched by league clubs whilst playing for the West Riding Under 19's and Keighley Central Youth club, He decided on joining Bradford City as an amateur in June 1958, and turned professional with The Bantams on his 17th Birthday in May 1960.

He left Valley Parade for Nottingham Forest in November 1961, but after just two years at the City Ground, Hockey was on the move again. This time he went to Newcastle United, where he collected a Second Division winner's medal in 1965.

Now transformed from a winger into a tough tackling central midfielder, Hockey joined Birmingham in November 1965 in a £25,000 deal.

Hockey spent five seasons at St Andrew's becoming a big favourite with the Blues fans for his aggressive displays and total committment.

Hockey went on to make 231 appearances for the Blues and scored 13 goals before he was transferred to Sheffield United for £35,000 in January 1971.

It is his time with Sheffield United, though, that saw him play at the height of his abilities.

He was brought in to revitalise the team when their game had begun to lack fire. They were in danger of missing out on promotion to Division One. His energetic displays played a large part in the United's promotion back to the top flight of English football.

His manager's instructions, "to battle, to win the ball, and give it to Tony Currie" paid dividends, and the two formed a memorable partnership. Hockey's Beatle-style haircut, distinctive headband, shaggy beard and tough tackling style singled him out as a cult-figure at Bramall Lane, and earning him a place in the hearts of those that saw him play. The remarks made by the manager, John Harris, to get the ball and give it to Currie was slightly wide of the mark. Hockey himself, an ex winger, could often beat his man, and his short and long passing was excellent.

His three seasons at Bramall Lane saw the Blades gain promotion and consolidate in the First Divison with two mid table finishes. Near the end of his third season, Hockey was dropped and put in a request for a transfer, it was accepted and he was part of an exchange deal that brought Jim Bone to Sheffield and saw Norwich City secure his services in February 1973. Trevor's stay at Norwich lasted just six months with Hockey going back to playing his football in Birmingham, this time at Villa Park.

After just a year at the Villa he was on the move again, this time returning to his first club Bradford City, where he finished his full time professional career.

Hockey was the first British player to make a full International appearance by virtue of his father's nationality rather than his own birthplace, when he gained the first of his nine caps for Wales.

In March 1976 Hockey became player-manager at Athlone Town before taking his footballing talents across the pond and a spell with San Diego Jaws in the North American Soccer League.

Hockey returned to England the following year and took on the manager's role at non-league Stalybridge Celtic before a further spell in the States as coach with both San Jose Earthquakes and Los Angeles Quicksilvers.

Trevor Hockey sadly died of a heart attack shortly after taking part in a five-a-side tournament in Keighley on 2nd April 1987, aged just 43.

Programme: Sheffield United versus Manchester United - Hockey had a splendid game as the Blades gained a 1-0 victory

United

Sheffield

Gil **Reece**

Gilbert Ivor Reece was born in Cardiff in July 1942. He was a Cardiff boy by birth and wanted to play his football for his hometown club. Which youngster doesn't want to play for the team he supports? Gil was proceeding along the right tracks, selected for his city and county sides. He then reached the pinnacle claiming a Welsh schoolboy cap, at outside left.

Unfortunately for Gil, after a short spell at Cardiff City, the club did not rate him that highly and he played his early adult football with Pembroke Borough, where he was spotted by the Newport County scouts.

So his first foray into league football came with a Welsh club, but not the one he would have liked. It could be said he was a late starter for he was 21 years old when he made his Newport County debut against Workington in the fourth division game in October 1963.

Reece had just 18 months at Newport County and scored 9 goals in his 32 first team appearances, before Sheffield United offered the Welsh club £10,000 for his services, which they accepted. The transfer took place in May 1965, just too late for Reece to make a division one appearance, but he did turn out in the County Cup Final and scored two goals in a 4-0 victory over Doncaster Rovers.

So just before his 23rd birthday Gil had won his first trophy, albeit, a local cup; risen from the fourth division to the top flight; was going on a tour of Latin America with his new side; and would start the next season playing against the likes of Manchester United, Arsenal, Spurs and Liverpool. Not a bad set of birthday gifts.

His first full season for the Blades was a very similar return as his Newport time with 32 games played and 8 goals scored. Basically the move up three divisions had made no difference to Reece and he helpd United claim ninth spot in the top division.

Reece had a traumatic season the following year when he broke his leg playing against Blackpool early in the season. He only managed 15 league games scoring four times.

Season 1967-68 was to see United relegated and only claim 32 points all season, but it was to be Reece's best season so far. He scored 13 goals in 35 games and was the club leading scorer. His nearest rivals, Addison, Hill and Woodward only had six strikes, each, to their name.

The following season saw Arthur Rowley take charge and make some significant changes. But old Arthur was a fan of Gil's style of play and made him a permanent fixture in the team.

United were trying to get back to the top flight of English football and made a good fist of it in season 69-70. Rowley's team started the season, but unfortunately the man himself didn't. Rowley was sacked just days before the season and Harris took the mantle once again. But whoever was in charge must have thanked their lucky stars for having Gil in the side. Once again he played a big part in United's sixth position, scoring 15 goals in 43 games. Only Woodward bettered his tally.

Promotion, as expected, did come to Bramall Lane in season 1970-71 and Reece was superb, especially in the final run with five goals in the last five games of the season, which included four wins and a draw. One of those goals was a stunning diving header against Birmingham City.

Back in Division One Reece did not get the games he thought he deserved and although he played in all the pre season friendlies it was not until late October that he actually started a league game. The writting was on the wall for Reece and he only ever made 19 more starts for United over the next 2 seasons. Stewart Scullion's arrival was the main reason.

Gil at least got some satisfaction from his move out of Bramall Lane. He went back to Cardiff City, the club who had deemed him not good enough as a youngster. In his four years there also helped them to a promotion in season 1975-1976.

Gil Reece (Sheffield United & Wales)

Gil Reece appearing on a give away card

U n i t e d

S h e f f i e l d

Billy **Dearden**

The purchase of William Dearden was not seen, at first, as one of the best transfers the Sheffield United management had ever undertaken. He was supposed to be a bit of a crock in his days at Crewe, Oldham and Chester and an outside right to boot, one of the few positions totally tied down at the Lane with Alan Woodward in such fine form.

Bill Dearden (Sheffield United)

Dearden's football league record was only 31 goals in 167 games, not exactly awe inspiring. But thankfully, United manager, John Harris thought differently and Billy became a Blade at the beginning of 1970-71 season. Harris did make a positional change, putting Dearden at Centre Forward.

After not being involved in the first game of the season, a game which was lost 3-1 at Leyton Orient. Billy replaced United's scorer in that first game, Colin Addison, and only missed one more league match all season, playing 40 games and scoring 14 goals, making him United's second top scorer. An excellent return of goals after stepping up in class by a few divisions. The fact that Dearden scored against Sheffield Wednesday in the 3-2 win, early in the season, made him a fan's favourite from almost the start of his stay at the Lane. His goals, that season, also propelled United into the top two places and promotion was gained.

The following season, in Division One, Dearden played 35 games and scored 16 league goals and finished club top scorer. A rise of four divisions in class and Billy was scoring more goals. United managed to finish 10th in that first season back in the top flight of English football. Dearden scored a hat-trick against West Ham United, a brace against Huddersfield and 11 single goal strikes against such sides as Leeds, Spurs, Forest, Man City, Wolves.

Season 1972-73 saw United only manage 14th place but once again Dearden's ratio was bettered, this time playing 37 games and returning 20 goals. No hat-tricks this time but he managed a brace of goals on 4 occasions against Southampton, WBA, Derby County and Spurs. He, also, scored the only goal of the game against Arsenal. The following season was to be his last under the manager who bought him from Chester, John Harris. The new manager, Ken Furphy, who took over in December only played Dearden four times. Billy did fight his way back into the side the following season, when United finished 6th in Division One, and played in 31 league games scoring 11 league and cup goals.

Unbelievably, the year that followed United's best season for a decade was their worst ever in repect of points gained. In fact, half the season had been played and they had only gained five points. Dearden only managed seven games with one goal, that coming against Manchester United. These games were under new manager Jimmy Sirrel who came in after Ken Furphy had been dismissed in October. The season was not helped by injuries to John Flynn and suspension of Tony Currie for the early part of the season, but it must be said the hierachy had let the team become old together with no real thought on purchasing Division One class players or developing the youth policy that used to by synonymous with Sheffield United.

So in 1976 Billy was released on loan back to his old club Chester and later he would return there on a free transfer. He carried on his career with further stints at Chesterfield and Mansfield where he had a spell as caretaker manager in 1983 and many years later in 1999 he went back to Field Mill as full time manager.

So that was the rollercoaster five years that Bill Dearden spent at Sheffield United coming in like a breath of fresh air with his goals. He played 175 league games and scored 61 goals - just over a goal every 3 games. His arrival and departure from and to Chester City were both low key, but his time under John Harris was anything but. His goals helped United to promotion to the top flight and when there propelling them into their highest position, 6th, for the last 30 years.

Bill Dearden appearing on a give away card from that era

United

Sheffield

Tony **Currie**

Tony Currie had trials in his youth with both Chelsea and Queens Park Rangers and was deemed not quite up to league standard by both clubs. It was left to Watford to give a young Currie his league chance. The management at Sheffield United had been keeping an eye on the youngster and had even come to an agreement with Watford in season 1967-68 that when the north London club was eliminated from the FA Cup, United would be allowed to sign Currie for an agreed fee of £26,500. Two asides to this little story are that United were the ones to knock Watford out of the Cup and that Watford were good to their word and did not try to up the price. After the agreed price was set, Currie gained youth international honours and was fast becoming a Watford cult figure, even at that early age.

So, in February 1968 Tony Currie signed for the Blades and went straight into the side that was struggling at the wrong end of the Division One table. He not only inspired United to a fine 3-2 home win over Spurs but also notched a debut goal, a rare header. He played in 13 league games in all and scored four goals, but could not stop United's slide into the second division of English football.

The next season 1968-69 was a settling period for United and a finish of ninth in the league was as good as the Blades could manage. Currie made 35 appearances but only managed four goals.

The following two seasons produced some excellent times for the United fans with finishes of sixth and second respectively. Currie never missed a league match in both these seasons and scored 12 and 9 goals. The 1970-71 season saw United gaining home attendances of around the 40,000 mark for their promotion run in. Over 87,000 Sheffielders saw the two derby games when United drew away at Hillsborough and won 3-2 at the Lane. The young Currie, still only just 21, was now pulling all the strings from midfield. He could pass long or short, had marvellous ball control and was very difficult to disposses. He also weighed in with more that a fair share of goals for a midfielder. Most of his goals were powerfully hit shots from outside the penalty area.

The next few seasons saw United placed around mid table with early exits in the FA Cup in both seasons. Season 1974-75 saw a nice upturn in fortune for United with a placing of sixth in Division One, finishing only four points behind the eventual champions Derby County. This high position coincided with Currie playing in every league game and scoring eight goals.

Tony could sometimes take his entertaining of the fans too far and the occasional wave or blowing kisses after beating an opponent was deemed by some to be disrespectful of fellow players. He was also criticised by his manager for not putting enough into his training. To try to counterbalance this seeming lack of enthusiasm, Ken Furphy, the manager, made Tony Currie captain of United. This was in place of Eddie Colquhoun and in hindsight was probably a mistake.

Sadly, Currie's last term was also United worst season, points wise, with only 22 points gained for the whole of the year. Currie, himself only managed one goal. In fact, only two United players managed to score more than three league goals. Relegation was assured and a player of Currie's ability is always desired elsewhere so the inevitable happened. He was transferred, unfortunately to Leeds United, for a fee of around £245,000.

At Leeds, Tony won another ten England caps and played there until his transfer to Queens Park Rangers in 1979. Tony managed a F A Cup final appearance in 1982 for the London club, then managed by Terry Venables. They gained a creditable draw with Spurs but lost in the replay, a game in which Currie was captain.

He was transferred to Vancouver Whitecaps and also played in Toronto before returning to the minor leagues of English football.

Tony Currie made over 340 league and cup appearances for Sheffield United and scored 61 goals in his eight years at Bramall Lane. He also gained seven England caps whilst a Blade.

Tony Currie signed Sheffield United programme

United

Sheffield

Keith **Edwards**

Keith Edwards was one of those players who could get into goalscoring positions with ease. He never seemed to struggle at any of his clubs to find the back of the net.

His goals' tally would have been phenomenal had he taken all his chances. He probably missed three times as many as he scored, but this is testament to the positional sense he had as a predator. He was lightening quick around the penalty area.

Edwards was born in Stockton on Tees in 1957. After a trial with Middlesborough in the mid 1970s which was not a success, he was spotted by Sheffield United scouts playing for his local side. He was asked to played for United's reserve eleven and scored two goals. His performance merited an offer from the club and he was immediately signed by the Blades manager, Ken Furphy. Unfortunately, Furphy was out of a job within a couple of weeks and Edwards was now under the guidance of Jimmy Sirrel.

Keith made his league debut in the disasterous relegation season, playing in three league games and not scoring. The following season in division two he was selected for 30 games and amazingly scored 18 goals. In eight consecutive games near the end of the season he bagged 11 goals. Only Alan Woodward scored into double figures, with 10 strikes.

In season 1977-78 his tally was not as good with only 11 goals from 32 starts. This was probably due to the fact he played under three managers: Sirrel, Coldwell and Haslam, the last playing Edwards more from the bench.

Haslam, obviously, did not rate Edwards that highly and let him go to Hull City for a fee of about £50,000. United then proceeded to sink down the football league and in 1981 managed the unthinkable and dropped into Division Four.

Luckily, United had a new manager, Ian Porterfield, and he and new chairman, Reg Brearley, had a five year plan for the

return to the top division. As we all know the plan did not fulfill all its agenda, but it did get United out of the Fourth Division, and as Champions. First on Porterfield list was to get someone who could find the back of the net. Keith Edwards was persuaded to come back to the Lane, albeit for double the money United let him go for. He now cost £100,000. His goals, 36 in 43 games, made sure United only stayed in the basement division for one season.

After gaining promotion the team and the crowd thought another promotion might be on the cards. This was not so and United looked a little uncertain. They finished mid table with the crowd sizes diminishing the longer the season went on. Edward managed 18 league and cup goals.

The malaise seemed to lift from Bramall Lane in season 1983-84 with Edwards scoring 41 goals from 53 league and cup games. Colin Morris added 20 league goals as the Blades managed third spot in the league and gained promotion, the second under Ian Porterfield.

After promotion, United, once again, seemed to take a step backward and only managed 18th spot in Division Two. Edwards still managed to score 15 league and cup goals.

Even though United managed to up their performance and finish in 7th position the following season, it was not good enough to save Ian Porterfield. He was replaced in late January by Billy McEwan. It was the new manager who let Keith Edwards leave and head up to Leeds United for a fee of around £125,000.

Keith's record of 163 goals in 297 games is well over a strike every two games and puts him behind only Alan Woodward in United's post war scoring records.

The Golden Boot won by Keith Edwards for his scoring feats

S h e f f i e l d

Alex **Sabella**

Alejandro (Alex) Sabella was brought to Bramall Lane by manager Harry Haslam for a fee of around £155,000 in August 1978. He was 23 years old at the time. Haslam signed the talented Argentinian midfielder along with Pedro Verde*. Now, it would be fair to say that, while Sabella's silky skills sometimes shone brightly, poor old Verde's did not and he moved back to Argentina just before the Falklands conflict.

A friendly against River Plate, a team that included five of the 1978 World Cup winners, was played at Bramall Lane, August 30th, as part of the Sabella deal and a crowd of well over 20,000 fans saw the Argentinian club side beat the Blades 2-1.

Alex Sabella was played in either outside or inside left position and he provided some sparkling displays in those early days. Sabella's time in Sheffield may have been much more memorable had Haslam returned from Argentina with the other player he also wanted, instead of Verde - a brilliant 16 year old. However, the youngster was going to cost around

£350,000 on top of the £150,000 Sabella transfer fee. United could not afford this, so the deal fell through. This was a shame, because the kid was called Diego Maradona.

It did seem as though the fans were getting their own little bit of post World Cup fever. There was massive interest at the club because English teams didn't really sign foreign players in those days.

A near 20,000 crowd came to see Sabella's first league match at Bramall Lane and he obliged with some deft touches and also swung across the corner kick from which Simon Stainrod nodded home. But a few good early season results, such as a 1-0 defeat of Liverpool in the League Cup, did not get United enough points to stave off relegation and the

unthinkable prospect of two Sheffield sides in Division Three was about to happen.

Poor old Sabella, a young kid in a foreign country, was going to have to try his skills in the Third Division of English football. The muddy pitches of Millmoor or Field Mill would not have seemed a good prospect for the young lad who was more used to playing on firm sun dried pitches, not to mention the daunting task of taking on some of the more aggresive right backs of the lower division.

Sabella – who would have looked like a world beater in most teams – playing without shin pads with his socks rolled down and beating his marker with ease – played 37 league games in the Third Division before Leeds United stepped in and saved him more ingnominy. Luckily, and as if to ease the blow for Sheffield United, the £400,000 transfer fee was well in excess of what the Blades had initially paid for Sabella's services.

His spell at Leeds was even shorter than with the Blades, with only 22 league appearances and just two goals. The Leeds United manager, Allan Clarke, decided Alex was not the kind of player he wanted in his team.

So in January 1982 Alex Sabella's four year stay in England came to an end when he was transferred, for a fee of £120,000, back to Argentinian club, Estudiented. The move was definitely good for Sabella who went on to gain full international honours with his home country. He was capped four times. He, later, moved to Brazilian club, Gremio, before finally seeing out his career back home in Agentina.

Alex Sabella was a little bit of an enigma with Sheffield United and for that matter Leeds as well, but you could see that the youngster had talent in abundance. He was probably with Sheffield United at a time in their history when his type of player was no use to the scrapping displays that were needed to keep the team from dropping further down the leagues.

*Pedro Verde is Juan Sebastian Veron's uncle.

Sheffield United versus River Plate programme

United

Sheffield

Tony **Agana**

Anthony Agana was born on 2nd October 1963 in Bromley, Kent. He was noticed as a schoolboy by Charlton Athletic and was on their books, but did not make a big enough impact to be signed on a permanent basis. He also had trials with Luton Town. He then settled into part time football with Weymouth and gained semi professional England international honours. Dave Bassett, than manager of Watford, spotted Agana and for a small transfer fee took him to the North of London club.

Tony Agana was obviously deemed a good prospect by Dave Bassett, the new United manager, because within six month of coming to the Blades, Dave had gone back to sign Agana from Watford in early 1988.

Agana played in 12 of the last 13 games as United battled to avoid relegation. They failed. Agana must have wondered if he had made the correct decision coming up north to Sheffield United.

Season 1988-89 saw United gain promotion and Tony Agana (29 goals) formed a strike partnership with Brian Deane (30 goals) that was to become the best pairing for over 60 years. Season 1927-28 had seen Harry Johnson and Fred Tunstall score 63 times.

Agana had a wonderful turn of speed and could leave defenders trailing in his wake. With Deane alongside him, almost any ball could be played from midfield or defence. The long ball could be chased and invariably led to a strike at goal. The short pass to feet was dealt with equally adeptly. Both players could hold the ball until a teammate became available.

Whilst both at their peak and injury free, they were a rare sight to behold. One game against Chester City in September 1988 saw both strikers notch hat-tricks in a 6-1 thumping of the Cheshire side. Agana also scored a hat-trick in the last home match of the season against Swansea City in a 5-1

victory. United scored over 90 goals and gained promotion to Division Two.

The following season, some fans thought United might have a side capable of pushing for promotion again. They were proved to be correct as the Blades sailed through the season and only failed to win the Second Division Championship on goal difference from Leeds United. The front pairing was not as fruitful as the previous year but still managed 34 goals between them. Agana scored two goals in that memorable last match of the season, away, at Leicester City. Sheffield United took so many amazingly attired fans to Leicester that day it seemed like a colourful home match.

Tony started to struggled with injuries and only managed 11 league appearances and two goals in season 1990-91 in Division One.

Tony played in 13 games at the start of Season 1991-92 and scored four times before Dave Bassett decided an offer from Notts County was too good to turn down. County offered Sheffield United around £700,000 for Agana's services. Dave Bassett had probably seen enough to decide Tony was slightly injury prone and it must be said had lost that initial goalscoring touch that had endeared him to the fans. The deal Bassett did for Sheffield United was exeptionally good business.

Tony's time at Notts County was woeful. The team suffered two relegations before Agana was loaned out to Leeds United and then, eventually, sold to Hereford United.

He later moved from Hereford to Cliftonville. He also played for Leek Town and Guisley.

Tony's career total for Sheffield United was 144 league and Cup games played and 50 goals scored – 13 of these appearances were as a substitute.

Sheffield United's Tony Agana depicted on a Panini Card

Sheffield

Dane **Whitehouse**

Sheffielder Dane Whitehouse was born in October 1970 and was fourteen years old when he signed schoolboy forms with Sheffield United. He was still only a comparative youngster when he made his full first team debut for the Blades in October 1978, a day after his 18th birthday.

He had impressed the management team with his displays in his six central league appearances so much they gave him a first team run out. So, Whitehouse had been involved, albeit briefly, in the promotion season into Division Two. He managed five league games; many more were to follow.

The next season was a joy to behold. Promotion was won once again; this time up to Division One. Dane was showing more composure on the ball and he was given more games as a reward. He managed 13 league and cup games – he even scored his first league goal, in a 4-1 away win at Bradford City.

As Sheffield United tried to consolidate their position in the top flight it was hard to give the younger players as free a rein as would normally be allowed. Whitehouse only made four appearances. Season 1991-92 was to see Whitehouse force his way into the first team reckoning with a few good goals in the pre season friendlies. He played in 34 league games, including nine as substitute, and scored eight goals.

The next season, 1992-93, saw the start of the English Premier League, and Whitehouse started in a good vein of form. Sadly, in early October he broke his shin. After his recovery, he forced his way back into the team that was to play Blackburn Rovers in the last eight of the FA Cup. United had beaten Manchester United in the previous round. Dane was selected in a more defensive role, playing left back, or at least starting the game in the number three shirt.

A good display against Blackburn saw a 0-0 draw. The replay went to penalties, after a 2-2 draw and United winning 5-4.

Whitehouse was now back to his old form and was soon playing on the left wing, again. The win over Blackburn Rovers in the 6th round deemed

United would now play the old enemy, Wednesday, in the semi-final. This was played out at Wembley.

Over 75,000 fans made their way to Wembley in April, for a game that will live long in the memory of all who were there.

Alan Cork's equaliser gave the Blades the impetus for the last part of the 90 minutes. Sadly, Mark Bright headed the winner for Wednesday in extra time.

After that Wembley disappointment, Sheffield United only lost one game out of the next eight. In fact they won their last three Premier League games. Whitehouse scored six times in his depleted season of only 18 appearances.

Dane Whitehouse was now back to his best, tracking up and down the left hand side of United's team. He helped out in defence as well as producing skillful crossing and wing play when attacking.

Sadly, the following season seemed to have a pall over it from the beginning of August. Brian Deane had already been sold in July, without the manager's consent. The replacement only managed nine goals, and unusually United had five players sent off. The foreboding came to a terrible conclusion when, somehow, the Blades ended up relegated.

Whitehouse, now free of injury, was a regular and appeared in 39 league games for United and scored 10 goals. A similar season followed with Dane playing 38 games, only this time he only managed six goals.

Season 1996-97 saw United reach the play-off final, versus Crystal Palace, at Wembley but sadly they came away with nothing.

A year later, United qualified, once again, for the play off games but Dane Whitehouse would never get to play in them. In fact, during a league game in November a dreadful tackle by a Port Vale player ended Dane Whitehouse's career. United helped Dane through the rehabilitation and back to what was deemed to be full health but he could not make that step back in to the top level of football.

Whitehouse, a young man who was playing at the top of his game and had turned down offers to move to bigger clubs was just 27 years of age when his career was cut short.

A benefit match, for Dane, was played at Bramall Lane in May 2001.

Nationwide Player of the Month Trophy which Whitehouse won for September 1996

U n i t e d

Sheffield

Brian **Deane**

Brian, whose family are originally from Nevis, an Island that is part of the Leeward group in the Caribbean, was born in Leeds in February 1968.

Deane started his Football League career as a part timer at Doncaster Rovers in season 1985-86. He played three games with no goals scored. He played another two seasons with Rovers, managing 63 more games and scoring 12 goals. These did not seem good statistics for a front man but Dave Bassett obviously saw something in the big striker that made him think Deane could do a job at Sheffield United.

Bassett proved his managerial credentials by once again spotting a "good un". In his five full seasons at Bramall Lane, Brian managed to score 30, 23, 16, 16 and 19 goals respectively.

In those early days his partnership with Tony Agana had to be seen to be believed. They tore defences apart: speed, power, pace, heading ability and powerful shooting. It was a little reminicant of the mid sixties when Jones and Birchenall exploded on to the Bramall Lane scene.

But Deane and Agana were far more prolific scorers than the two blonde striker of yesteryear. With 59 goals between them in that first season as a partnership, it looked like the Blades manager Bassett had found two excellent young strikers

who might well develop together.

Deane was the main man in this pairing, although in that first season, the 59 goals were split evenly with Deane just edging it to score 30.

Deane carried on being the more prolific of the pair and after two seasons, carrying unfortunate injuries, Tony Agana was transferred to Notts County in a very good piece of business by Bassett.

Brian had obviously been watched on a few occasions by England and was duly honoured with three England caps on a tour of New Zealand.

Deane was aided in the goalscoring efforts by Whitehouse, Bryson and Littlejohn. But none of these players ever reached double figures with United. Deane, for a couple of seasons, did seem to be ploughing a lone furrow up front.

In season 1992-93 when the English First Division changed to the Premiership format, Brian was the first man to score a goal. It is a record he can be proud of.

Brian Deane had always carried on scoring at a very good rate of goals per game and it was not unexpected when Leeds United came in for him. What was rather unexpected, though, is that the player was sold whilst the manager, Bassett, was out of the country. He obviously knew nothing about the deal. When he returned to be told of the transfer, it is said Bassett told the United Chairman that relegation would come at the end of the year. It did.

Brian went on to become a favourite at Elland Road, although never scoring at the same rate as his Sheffield days.

Nigel Spackman was now in charge at Bramall Lane and he decided to fetch Deane back to Sheffield United. He paid somewhere in the £1m range and the fans were pleased to see a hero return. Brian showed good figures with 11 goals jn 24 games and played alongside another good striker in Fjortoft. Deane was being touted by Portugese side, Benfica, and in January he was sold to everybody's disbelief. When the second striker Fjortoft was sold, the similarity with the Jones and Birchenall affair of 30 years earlier once again sparked the unrest of the fans.

Deane came back to England with Middlesbrough where he stayed for four seasons before moving to Leicester City for a couple of years. Brian is now back helping the Blades try for promotion, although he has not appeared in the first team. Yet!

Brian Deane defending! Sheffield United versus Leeds – a sports postcard

60

United

Sheffield

Alan **Cork**

Of all the players selected in this book, it is probably Alan Cork who has turned out in the least number of games for Sheffield United. He only made 25 starting league appearances for the Blades. He made more appearances as a substitute. He managed 29 games, when coming on from the bench. He scored seven times in the league and twice in the FA Cup.

But it is his goal in the 1993 Semi Final of the Cup that gets Cork a place in Sheffield United's history books. It was a goal against, local rivals, Sheffield Wednesday, in a big cup game and it just seemed to catch the moment of the game and the

season. The Sheffield United fans noisily came alive with Corky running around Wembley with both hands aloft with that bearded smile just before he and Franz Carr danced and hugged one another in sheer delight.

The fans were cheering and United had pegged Wednesday back to 1-1 after Waddle's free kick had given the Owls the lead. The FA Cup Final was within reach.

A battle royal commenced and both sides could have won the day and gone on to face Arsenal in the final. The game was into extra time when Mark Bright ended the Blades hopes with a downward header that evaded Kelly in the United net.

Sadly, it was not to be United's first return to a Wembley final for over 50 years.

It should also be remembered that Alan Cork did his bit towards getting to that Steel City semi final at Wembley when he scored the only goal of the game to help Sheffield United overcome Hartlepool United in a fourth round tie at the Lane. He also scored one of United's five penalties, that took the

Blades through, against Blackburn Rovers in the sixth round shoot out after their two drawn games.

Alan Cork was born in 1959 and did not come to Sheffield United until just after his 32nd birthday. He had played for Wimbledon for 15 seasons managing over 400 games and well over 140 goals. His career did not start at the London club though. His first league club was Derby County. He never actually played in the first team with County and moved to Lincoln City in 1977 on loan, playing five games. He was then transferred to Wimbledon in season 1977-78.

When Cork was brought to Bramall Lane by Dave Bassett, his first game was coming on from the subs bench in the Derby game against Sheffield Wednesday on 11th March 1992. The game resulted in a 3-1 away win for the Blades with Bobby Davison (two) and Dane Whitehouse scoring the United goals.

Dave Bassett bought Alan Cork for Sheffield United Football Club to do a specific job. He was a robust and bustling type of player who could be called on for the last 15 to 20 minute period to go in and ruffle a few feathers in the opponents' defence. The United boss knew it was a short term deal as Alan Cork himself was not really up to the rigours of the Premiership on a full 90 minute basis. But it took a little of the weight off Brian Deane who, since Agana's departure, had really been the lone marksman in the United side. Cork's age was also a factor in the, mostly, late substitutions.

Alan Cork, despite his age, did work hard at trying to win the fans over, he never gave less than a 100% commitment and was a good player at holding the ball, so the midfielders could be brought into the game when a long ball had been punted up to the front men. He also, occasionally, showed some of that Wimbledon agression that made one or two referees have a quiet word with him.

Alan Cork was transferred to Fulham in August 1994

Sheffield United versus Sheffield Wednesday FA Cup Semi Final programme 1993

United

Sheffield

Nathan **Blake**

Nathan Blake was released and given a free transfer by his first club, Chelsea, when he was only 18 years of age. This was a devastating blow for a young man to handle but at his new, less fashionable, club Cardiff City he won over the supporters and helped the Bluebirds gain two promotions. Nathan played for the Welsh club over 130 games and scored 35 goals.

Sheffield United stepped in to the transfer market and offered Cardiff City £300,000 for Blake's services. The clubs and player agreed term. Nathan became a Blade on 17th February 1994.

His stay at Bramall Lane did not please a certain section of the fans. Blake was expected to help keep United in the Premiership with a hat full of goals. His first four games were as a substitute and he managed two goals. His late purchase that season really meant he had no time to settle into the side and show what he could achieve. He started seven games and made five substitute appearances, scoring five times. Too little, too late. The year ended, very badly, and relegation became certain as everyone listened to the 4.45pm results on the last Saturday of season 1994. How did Everton win that game?

Nathan Blake managed to score 17 times in the following season as he slowly started to win the supporters over. United's effort of 8th place was not really good enough though.

Season 1995-96 was difficult, to say the least, and Dave Bassett resigned. And with terms like "no hunger or determination" being bandied around just before new man Howard Kendall arrived, it seemed as though another season would be wasted. Blake, at least, was starting to look the part: 20 starts and 12 goals. At least United had someone who could find the net!

Well, it seemed as though Howard Kendall did not think too highly of Blake and within a week of Dave Bassett resigning Blake was on his was to Bolton. Now it must be said it was good business in the money sense paying £300,000 for the player and selling him for four times as much, £1,250,000. But no matter what the price sometimes you have to hang on to the players who may, just, be able to swing a season your way with his goals.

Blake, as stated, departed in December. At that stage he had scored 12 times. By the end of the season, four months later, he was still the leading scorer by four goals. Andy Walker was his nearest challenger with eight strikes.

Nathan Blake played only 55 full league games for Sheffield United scoring 34 times. He played in 4 cup matches and scored once.

Blake was to have a torrid few seasons at his new club Bolton.

His first season did not go well. He scored only one goal in 18 outings. Bolton Wanderers were relegated. In the following season, he was much better, scoring 19 times, as Bolton bounced straight back up to the Premiership. He scored 12 goals the next season as Bolton took on the mantle of the YoYo team as they were, once again, relegated.

Part way throught the next season Blackburn Rovers came in for Blake and paid a staggering £4,250,000 for his services. Sadly, he did not repay that vast sum. He scored only 13 goals in his 54 games at the Ewood Park club. He was sold to Wolves for £1,500,000, a huge loss of £3,000,000.

Three seasons with Wolves showed far better returns with 25 goals in 78 games. He then moved to Leicester City where in 14 games he never found the oppositions net.

He played on loan at Leeds United for two games and scored once. Blake was released by Leicester in June 2005.

Nathan played for his country, Wales, 29 times, scoring four goals. He also scored 167 league and cup goals in a career spanning 15 years.

Nathan Blake pictured after scoring his first goal for Sheffield United

United

Sheffield

Alan **Kelly**

Alan Kelly was born in Preston in August 1968 and some 20 years later he was to follow in his father's footsteps and play for the Lancashire club. At Preston North End Kelly made over 150 appearances but was transferred to Sheffield United in 1992.

Alan Kelly was a top class Sheffield United goalkeeper, possibly good enough to be mentioned in the same breath as Hodgkinson and Foulke. His signing from Preston North End was an excellent piece of transfer market dealing, by manager Dave Bassett. At a final transfer cost of about £200,000, Kelly was a snip, especially when the likes of Chris Woods cost a cool one million pound around the same time. At the age of just 24 he still may have had 10-12 years left in the game. Hopefully, all of them at Sheffield United.

Kelly was an astonishing shot stopper and gave some remarkable displays for United. It seemed on some Saturday afternoons he was salvaging a point for the Blades almost single handedly.

In one on one situations with an attacking forward he always looked as though he would come out second best, slightly slow, but he was deceptive! He always seemed to come out of these situations with the ball. He was a remarkably tough individual who would go into the goalmouth melee when some keepers might use judgement that would see them go in feet first or perhaps not at all. He was an extremely brave goalkeeper.

He was capped by The Republic of Ireland on a number of occasions and never seemed to let them down. He was second in line behind Pat Bonner for quite a few years, and to be honest he was much the better keeper. He was an Ireland squad member for two World Cup Finals.

Alan will probably be remembered by the Lane fans for his penalty saves against Blackburn Rovers in the quarter finals of the FA Cup in 1993. Taking them through to the Steel City Semi Final played at Wembley stadium, where they lost 2-1 in extra time. He was influential in Sheffield United making their way to another FA Cup semi final in 1998. When they met Newcastle United at Old Trafford and lost 1-0.

Sadly, for United, Kelly was lured by the offer of a Blackburn Rovers contract only a couple of seasons after the Ewood Park club had been Premiership Champions. United were playing out their games in Division One and you can understand why Kelly thought a move up the footballing ladder would benefit his game, as well as his salary.

Kelly departed from Bramall Lane in 1999 and went to

Blackburn Rovers where he and John Filan vied for the first team jersey for a while. Blackburn manager Graeme Souness thought he needed a larger figure in the net and as he had Jack Walkers' cash behind him he bought USA keeper Brad Friedel. Therefore limiting Kelly's first team appearances.

It was rumoured that in 2000, Manchester United wanted to sign Alan Kelly when they had two keepers injured and were due to play Bayern Munich in the Champions League. In the end they purchased Andy Goram, ex Glasgow Rangers and Scotland keeper.

Alan Kelly did move out from Blackburn, on loan, to Stockport County and also had a six game loan spell at Birmingham City.

He stayed at Ewood Park as understudy to Brad Friedel, who was, and is, the most consistent goalkeeper in the Premiership. Kelly only played one league game in his last two seasons at Ewood Park.

Alan Kelly followed in his fathers footsteps by attaining league and international football status.

Alan Kelly, Republic of Ireland goalkeeper

United

S h e f f i e l d

Jan-Aage **Fjortoft**

Jan-Aage Fjortoft was purchased, by Howard Kendall, from Middlesbrough in late 1996 for a fee of around three quarters of a million pounds. He was allowed to leave the North East club and Sheffield United were lucky to get a current Norwegian international who was noted for being a sharp finisher. However, his overall work rate was a little questionable.

He started his first game, in February 1997, away, against Swindon Town. He must have thought he had made a serious mistake, United lost 2-1 and before a crowd of only 8,000. The next match, his home debut, was another defeat, against Norwich City. Thankfully, Fjortoft's scoring record (he scored 10 goals in 15 league games) was enough to see Sheffield United qualify for the end of season play-offs. The eventual winner of these play-offs games would gain a place in the Premier League. The games were over a two legged format.

Fjortoft managed a goal against Ipswich in the 1-1 home draw. He also made one of United's two goals that earned another draw at Portman Road. United went through on the away goals rule. It seemed as though the purchase of Fjortoft might pay the ultimate dividend.

The Play-Off final was against Crystal Palace who had defeated Wolverhampton Wanderers in their semi-final.

The game, at Wembley, was a scrappy affair with both sides seemingly incapable of scoring a goal. Sadly, for United, in the last minute of the match Carl Tiler headed the ball away and it fell straight to David Hopkins, the Welsh international. He struck the ball cleanly and it ended up in the top corner of the net giving goalkeeper and defenders no chance. Palace had gained promotion and United had to come away from London with nothing except the knowledge that another season in Division One awaited them.

Fjortoft played in the early games in season 1997-98 and scored 12 times in league and cup before, surprisingly, he was transferred to Barnsley. It is always a bad deal to sell a player whom the crowd have taken a shine to, but to sell him to a local side that is perceived to be doing better than your club is

asking for a backlash. This was about the same time as Deane was released to Benfica. Although Sheffield United picked up nearly £2,000,000 from the sale of these two players it not only undermined the team spirit but left the fans in shocked disbelief. Sadly, more unsettling news was to follow; Don Hutchison was allowed to go to Everton.

In fairness to the management team at the time, firstly Spackman and then Thompson, still managed to see United into the top six placings, and gain a play off place. However, United lost to Sunderland 2-0 after winning 2-1 at Bramall Lane and did not make it to Wembley.

Jan-Aage Fjortoft had played only 30 full league games and scored 19 league goals for United. In the FA Cup he managed two goals in two appearances. His record stands up well against any of the strikers who have graced the Bramall Lane pitch.

Born 10th January 1967, in Aalesund, Norway Jan-Aage Fjortoft played for Hamkam, Lillestrom, Rapid Vienna and Swindon Town. Jan joined Swindon Town at the beginning of their first ever season in the Premier League in 1993.

After a slow start for Swindon, he started to score prolifically, becoming a firm favourite with the fans, often scoring spectacular goals from impossible angles. In 1994, he became only the second Swindon Town player to play in the World Cup Finals whilst at the club, when he played for Norway.

He was bought from Swindon by Middlesbrough's Bryan Robson in April 1995 and sold by the same manager to Sheffield United on 31st January 1997. He then moved to Barnsley, staying about one year, before leaving for Eintracht Frankfurt in November 1998. The striker spent three seasons with the German outfit before heading home in 2001 to join Stabaek. In May 2002, he made one final switch to his former club Lillestrom, ending his playing career one month later. Fjortoft went on to work for Norwegian television before becoming general manager at Lillestrom in December 2004.

United

Sheffield

Michael **Brown**

Michael Brown was born in Hartlepool on January 25th 1977.

Michael was just 18 years old when he made his Premiership debut for Manchester City on 26th August 1995. He came on as a substitute in a 2-1 defeat at Coventry City.

Brown played 89 times for the Manchester club, scoring just two goals. Whilst at City he went on loan to Hartlepool, his home town, and Portsmouth. He played six games and scored one goal for Hartlepool and made four starts for Portsmouth without registering a goal.

Neil Warnock came into the post as Sheffield United Manager in December 1999 and bought Michael Brown, now aged 23 for a fee of around £400,000. Michael played his first game for United on 19/12/1999, against Blackburn. He was Neil Warnock's first permanent signing.

Strangely, as is the case in football, one of Michael's first games for Sheffield United, after his permanent signing was against his old side, Manchester City. He scored the only goal in a 1-0 win for United.

Michael played 21 full league games in that first season and scored three goals.

His next season 2001-2002 saw an improvement in games played. He managed 40 appearances but sadly only found the net on two occasions. His best was yet to come!

Brown seemed to thrive in the Sheffield United shirt and in the 2002-03 season he scored a magnificent 22 goals (in all competitions) from a central midfield position. His efforts helped United to the semi-finals of both domestic cups. They played and beat Liverpool in the first leg of the League Cup Semi Final but could not hold out as the Premiership side won 2-0 at

Anfield. They came up against the mighty Arsenal in the FA Cup semi-final and did themselves proud with a performance that had the Gunner's manager, Wenger, worried until a poor refereeing decision cost United dearly. The team also managed to get to the play off final at the Millennium Stadium, where they played Wolves. Unfortunately, Wolves started the game on time and United picked up the pace about 20 minutes later. By half time the Blades were doomed to another season in the second tier of English football.

Brown had been noticed by the Premiership clubs and they had been sniffing around Bramall Lane for the last few months of the season. When a player shows the type of goal return from midfield that Brown had been doing it is obvious the bigger clubs will come poaching. Michael got one of his better goals, a long range strike, against Sheffield Wednesday.

He played a dozen or so games the following season and scored two goals. Then, as expected, he was gone. The money clubs came hunting, and he was enticed to the capital.

Brown was bought from Sheffield United for around £500,000 by David Pleat the manager of Tottenham Hotspur. Brown proved a dependable if unspectacular player. His 46 appearances only showed four goals up until the end of the 2004-05 season. Although well liked by the Spurs fans for his hard work and aggresive contribution, the strengthening of the Spurs midfield under Martin Jol affected Brown's position. He could not fight his way past Edgar Davids, Michael Carrick or the rest to gain a permanent place in the Spurs starting line up.

On January 31, 2006 he left Tottenham Hotspur to make the short trip across London to sign for Chris Coleman and Fulham Football Club. He is currently playing first team football in the Premiership for the Craven Cottage club and looking to show the type of form that won him rave reviews whilst he was a Blade.

Michael Brown playing for Sheffield United against Fulham. Michael is now a Fullham player

United

Sheffield

Michael **Tonge**

Michael Tonge was born in Manchester on April 7th, 1983.

By the age of 15 he was being groomed at Manchester United Football Club. Sadly, with the abundance of talent at their beck and call Tonge was not deemed good enough for the Lancashire club. He moved to Sheffield United at the tender age of sixteen.

He played his first game for the Blades against Wimbledon on April 17th 2001, just after his 18th birthday. He signed full time for the club, a couple of months later, in July 2001.

He had captained the Sheffield United youth team and only played in the reserves for a few games before gaining and then holding on to a first team shirt.

A highly influential player, Michael Tonge operates in a central or wide midfield role and has made himself a key player in the Sheffield United set-up with over 200 League and Cup games and more than 20 goals for the Blades. This from a player who is still only 23 years old, is quite amazing. His pacy, talented performances led to an English youth international call-up.

Season 2002-2003 saw Sheffield United qualifying for both major cup semi-finals and the Blades seemed to be the most televised football team in England. A number of Premier sides

were sitting up and taking notice of a few of the Blades young players. Especially, Tonge, Jagielka and Brown.

With wins against Premiership sides: Sunderland, Liverpool and Leeds, twice, the bigger clubs started to sniff around Bramall Lane.

In the semi final first leg of the Worthington Cup, played at Bramall Lane, United took on the mighty Liverpool. Michael

Tonge scored two splendid goals to help Sheffield United to a stunning 2-1 win over one of Europe's top clubs. He also collected the man of the match award from Sky television for his efforts.

Here was a young man who was probably the best midfielder on show that night and imposed himself on the game more quickly and influentially than any of the internationals of the Merseyside club. Sadly, United lost 2-0 at Anfield and did not make the Worthington Cup Final.

That same season, 2002-2003, was to throw up some stunning games, especially the local Yorkshire derbies against Premiership side Leeds United. The Blades drew them in both cup competitions and duly defeated them, twice. Always a nice feeling to beat Leeds United.

After battling their way through to another semi-final, the FA Cup, United faced the undefeated Arsenal. This was going to be a tough game, but to be fair to United they looked the better side on the day and only a poor refereeing decision cost them the game.

After all the hard work in both cup competitions, where they played and beat four Premiership sides, the Holy Grail was still up for grabs in the First Division play off final at the Millennium Stadium in Cardiff.

The game itself, a defeat by Wolves, left a bitter taste, although, United should have been proud of what they achieved that season with so many young players in the squad.

That long hard season saw Tonge play in 58 league and cup games in which he scored eight goals.

Playing alongside the Scottish international Stuart McCall for a couple of seasons has most definitely helped Michael Tonge develop his game.

With promotion and the Premiership beckoning Michael Tonge will, hopefully, have a long and prosperous career at Sheffield United where he will go on to play many more games and, hopefully, gain further international honours.

Sheffield United programme - The Blade - showing Michael Tonge on the cover

Sheffield

Leigh **Bromby**

Leigh Bromby, the former Sheffield Wednesday and Norwich defender, was born in Dewsbury on June 2nd 1980.

He signed for Sheffield United on 24 May 2004 and made his debut at Burnley, 7th August the same year.

Leigh Bromby joined the Blades along with his Owls team mates Alan Quinn and Derek Geary, after the, then, Hillsborough manager Chris Turner decided to clear out his squad and released almost 20 players. Neil Warnock moved in quickly and signed three of the younger, better players on free transfers. The United boss showed awareness and did an excellent piece of transfer market business.

Leigh started his career across the city at Hillsborough and made his debut for Wednesday in December 2000.

His Football League debut, however, had come a year earlier on 12 December 1999. This was in a game for Mansfield Town against Barnet during a three month loan period. He played 11 league and cup games for Mansfield and also scored his first career goal in a 3-1 win over Southend United in January 2000.

After his loan period at Mansfield was over he gained a first team place back at Hillsborough and around Christmas 2000 he made his Wednesday debut in a 1-0 home defeat to Wolves.

The 2001/02 season was a poor year for both Sheffield sides with the Blades only finishing 13th and the Owls a lowly 20th. But at least Bromby was now playing regularly and appeared in the Sheffield derbies, which both ended scoreless. Wednesday reached the League Cup Semi-Final, losing to Blackburn Rovers 6-3 on aggregate.

The Owls were relegated the following season. It was during this season that Leigh Bromby got the first red card of his career in a 3-0 defeat at Wimbledon. He also had a loan spell at Norwich City for whom he played five games.

Leigh gave some impressive performances in what was a poor Owls side and he, supposedly, attracted the interest of Chelsea and Tottenham. Norwich, who he had been loaned out to, made an offer of £500,000 for his services.

Leigh stayed in the lower league one season and was then given a free transfer by manager Turner. Sheffield United manager, Warnock, stepped in quickly to clinch a deal that has given Sheffield United a very talented defender, as well as two Irish midfielders who can both command first team places when fit.

Bromby made his Sheffield United debut away at Burnley and has been man of the match in many of the games he has played since. His long throw-ins also give Sheffield United the capability of keeping a team under pressure when a ball goes out of play anywhere in the opposition half.

Usually players who make the risky move across the city football divide can expect some supporter criticism. But from the off, Leigh Bromby's sound displays have meant he has been well received by the Blades fans who have taken to his defensive work ethic. Unitedites now seem happy to point out to the Owls supporters that the Hillsborough mob sold a 'good un'.

He has got stronger over the last few years and is not as easily moved off the ball as was sometimes the case in his early years at Hillsborough. He has grown in physical stature and is now capable of taking on any of the opposition forwards, no matter what their size. He is a very capable defender who can play in any of the four positions across the back line. The present Sheffield United side do seem that little less mobile at the back without Bromby being in there.

Leigh Bromby seems to be a player who always enjoys his football. Long may that continue, hopefully, in a Sheffield United shirt.

Leigh Bromby was named HFS player of the year in 2005.

Signed photograph of Leigh Bromby

S h e f f i e l d

Paddy **Kenny**

Paddy Kenny was born on the 17th of May 1978 in the Yorkshire town of Halifax.

Paddy's goalkeeping prowess was spotted by Neil Warnock when he was brought to Bramall Lane from Bury for a loan spell near the end of the 2001-2002 season. Simon Tracey was coming to the end of his impressive Sheffield United career and Kenny was signed on a permanent basis, just before his 24th birthday, to fill the goalkeeping position. He has never looked back. From the start of his first team appearances he has never looked in any jeopardy of losing his position. Paddy rarely had a bad game, and when the odd poor display did come along he invariably followed them up by putting in a series of top notch displays. When he was injured in season 2003-2004, Paul Gerrard came in and did a very sound job for Sheffield United.

Before his transfer to Sheffield United, Paddy had played seven games for Whitby Town, in the lower leagues, in season 1998-99. He then appeared in over 120 league and cup games for Lancashire side, Bury between 1999 until his transfer to United in 2002.

Paddy realised he had made a good choice when Sheffield United managed semi final places in both domestic cups, FA and League, and made the Millennium Stadium for a play off final against Wolves. In that first full season Paddy was also voted the Supporters' Player of the Year.

Paddy has also followed in the footsteps of another of Sheffield United's previous goalkeepers, Alan Kelly, by gaining Republic of Ireland international honours.

Paddy Kenny, who qualifies via both his Irish born parents, declared himself happy to play for Ireland in late 2002.

The Blades keeper jumped ahead of the likes of Dean Kielly, (Charlton and Portsmouth), Graham Stack and Dean Delaney on the basis that he was playing regular football with his club, whereas others have found themselves mostly consigned to the bench. He still has to bypass one of the best keepers in the Premiership, Shay Given of Newcastle, to grab the number one spot for the Republic of Ireland. That position is something you would imagine Paddy still sees as a target, especially with the European Championships in two years time and the next World Cup only 4 years away. By 2010 Paddy will still only be 32 years of age, still a comparitively young age for a goalkeeper.

This season, 2005-2006, the former Bury number one has once again played a major part in the Blades rise to the top positions of the Championship, hopefully with promotion to the Premiership as his and the team's reward.

Paddy has been linked with a move to a couple of Premiership clubs in the past few seasons, but he has stayed loyal to the Blades, along with playing colleagues, Tonge and Jagielka who have also been the target for transfer speculation.

At one point there was slight confusion over contract negotiations but Paddy has now signed a deal that will, thankfully, keep him at Bramall Lane until 2009.

Paddy Kenny has all the attributes to take the mantle from Alan Kelly and progress into a top quality keeper for club and country. Playing for only four seasons he cannot be assessed, just yet, as to whether he will be as good as Kelly, Tracey, Hodgkinson, or Faulke. But he is definitely showing all the right signs.

Sheffield United's programme The Blade, January 2004 v West Ham, with Paddy Kenny pictured on the cover

Sheffield

Phil **Jagielka**

Phil Jagielka was born in Manchester on 17th August 1982.

Jagielka came through the youth set up at Bramall Lane and United are now reaping the full rewards of this young midfielder cum defender. He is a player who Neil Warnock can rely upon to do the business in whatever position he plays him.

Phil Jagielka is a player who has shown loyalty to the club that brought him through the ranks. There are clubs out there

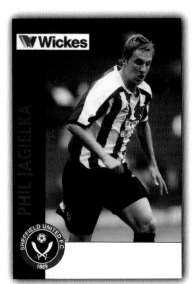

who are willing to pay very large sums of money, Wigan offered up to £5 million, for his services, which was thankfully turned down by the Blades. Bolton Wanderers have also been linked with Jagielka's signature.

He stated, on a local radion station, that he would like to stay at Sheffield United and repay the club who gave him the chance to shine in league football. Loyalty is not a word you hear too often these days, especially in the money laden world of football.

Warnock was pretty sure the Manchester youngster would make the grade and made sure the lad stayed at the club by offering him a three year deal before his eighteenth birthday.

In those early days he helped Sheffield United gain league and cup success at reserve and youth team level.

He is now an established first team player within the Sheffield United set up.

Jagielka has played well over 200 league and cup games, all in the Championship, and a step up to what is probably the best league in the world, The Premiership, can do his

blossoming footballing career nothing but good.

Jagielka is keen to prove he has what it takes to succeed in The Premiership. "I'd like to think I could cut it in The Premiership, I am desperate to get there," Jagielka told The Times in an interview in March 2006.

Midfielder Jagielka has been named Championship Player of the Year at the Football League awards. The awards ceremony, which took place in London in March 2006, saw Jagielka receive the award, being voted number one in a list of the top 50 players in The Football League by FourFourTwo magazine. Jagielka won ahead of last season's victor in Reading midfielder Steve Sidwell and Crystal Palace striker Andy Johnson.

He was also named the Sheffield United Supporters Club Player of the Year for the second successive year in March 2006. These awards show what a high level of performance he has been reaching on a regular basis.

For the last three years Phil Jagielka has averaged over 50 games per season.

With younger player like Jagielka, Tonge, Bromby, Kenny, Webber, Quinn and experienced pros like Morgan, Unsworth and Shipperly, the cornerstone for Sheffield United's future is already in place. The Blades, hopefully, can develop like Charlton, Wigan, Bolton and West Ham United who all managed to gain promotion and then consolidate a Premiership place.

Phil Jagielka has gained England international honours at Under 17 and England Under-21 level. It was at the Under 21 level that he scored one of the goals in a 2-0 victory over Slovakia at the Stadium of Light.

His older brother Steve was also a professional footballer at Shrewsbury Town.

Advertising postcard showing Phil Jagielka

United

United players who nearly made the list

Alan Birchenall was a bit like the buses we all wait for, none for ages then two at the same time. This was the scenerio with Mick Jones and Alan Birchenall both arriving roughly at

Alan Birchenall (Sheffield United)

the same time and looking as though United's goalscoring problems would be solved for many years to come. Birchenall arrived on the scene against Stoke City in an away game in September 1964, Jones scoring the only goal of the game. The next game, also away, against Sheffield Wednesday saw the young striker bag both goals in United's 2-0 victory. In the next 11 games the United fans thought the motherload had been found with these two blonde forwards scoring 17 goals between them, culminating in a 4-0 victory over Arsenal when they both scored two goals each. Sadly, this type of feat did not carry on and end of season figures of 13 goals for Birchenall and 17 for Jones, although solid was not what that early pairing had

promised. The next two years showed an improvement for Jones's tally but sadly Birchenall only managed ten goals in each season. The relegation season of 1968 still rankles with United fans when both Jones, (to Leeds United) and Birchenall, (to Chelsea), were sold within months of each other, albeit for £100,000 each. The season's last game was at home against Chelsea, Birchenall's new side, the Blades lost 2-1 and relegation was assured.

Brian Gayle was signed for Sheffield United in 1991 when the team was at the bottom of Division One, with only one win to their name. Dave Bassett took a big gamble on signing Gayle from Ipswich Town. Not just because any player you buy for £750,000 is a risk but for the fact that the manager personally loaned the club £100,000 to complete the deal. Gayle did not let Sheffield United or Bassett down. In fact, he probably repaid the transfer fee in full in that first season, leading the team from bottom spot up to ninth position by the end of the season. United had

Brian Gayle (Sheffield United)

only gained five points from their first eight games before Gayle was moved in to the centre of the Blades defence. He was the United captain for the FA Cup, Steel City, semi final which took place at Wembley in 1993 and was unlucky to be on the losing side. After only 117 league games and nine goals an arthritic problem put paid to a career that should have gone on for longer. He tried his luck in the lower divisions but it was a losing battle.

He started his professional career at Wimbledon and was unlucky not to feature in their cup final side of 1988 when they beat Liverpool. He moved to Manchester City for a fee in excess of £300,000 and helped the Maine Road side secure promotion to Division One. Unfortunately for Brian the new manager Howard Kendall did not rate him that highly and let him go to Ipswich from where United bought him.

Bob Booker gave United three seasons of commitment and effort, probably unequalled in the last twenty years by any player. He came to Sheffield United from Brentford when aged nearly 31 and played in over 120 games, scoring on 13 occasions. He had played for Brentford for eleven seasons and was about to sign for Barnet when United's Simon Webster was injured. Dave Bassett went looking for a quick replacement and he chose Booker. It took Bob a few games to win the fans over, but this he did. He was a wholehearted tryer. A never say die attitude is not really a substitute for ability but with his experience, albeit of lower league soccer, he played a big part in United promotion in

Bob Booker (Sheffield United)

season 1989-90 playing 38 games and scoring eight times. He was also captain for the last three games of the season in Stancliffe's absence. What a day it must have been for Booker when United won the last game of the season to make sure of promotion 5-2 away at Leicester City. Two years earlier he was going to settling for playing part time football and setting up a contract cleaning business. Booker played over 40 Division One games over the next two seasons and just before his 34th birthday he moved back to Brentford. A knee injury ended his playing career but he became coach at the north London club before moving on to Brighton to become assistant manager.

Gerry Summers was born in 1933 in the Small Heath part of Birmingham and joined West Bromwich Albion from school. It took Summers seven years to break into the West Brom side and he made his debut in December 1955. He could not command a regular place as he was reserve to Ray Barlow, the incumbent English international, so when the chance arose to move to United in 1957 he accepted. He was the last piece in Joe Mercer's defence and for six years was an automatic first team choice at Bramall Lane. Even though Gerry's first four seasons were played in the Second Division, United regularly reached the latter stages of the FA Cup. In his first season, 1957-58, United reached the last 16 losing to Summer's old club West Brom, after a replay. The following two seasons they went one better and reached the last eight losing to Norwich and Sheffield Wednesday respectively. Season 1960-61 brought promotion and an even better showing in the FA Cup, a semi final appearance against Leicester City. After two goalless draws and missing a penalty in the third game, United lost out and Leicester went on to Wembley.

Gerry Summers (Sheffield United)

Summers helped United to fifth in 1962, their highest position for many years and not bettered since. He played two more seasons, both, mid table finishes, before he moved on to Hull City in 1964.

U n i t e d

Don Hutchison started his playing career with his local club Hartlepool United in 1990. After less that a year Liverpool had moved in quickly and picked Hutchison up for a transfer fee of £175,000, which was a considerable sum for a youngster with so few league appearances.

He was not an automatic choice at Anfield, but he did make nearly 50 starts in his four years on Merseyside.

Liverpool did excellent business on the Gateshead born player when selling him to West Ham United for over £1.5 million.

He was signed by United manager Howard Kendall, for Sheffield United from West Ham on 12th January 1996 for a fee in excess of £1,000,000 making him United's record buy.

He made his debut for the Blades against Tranmere in an away game. He played around 80 games for Sheffield United and scored six goals. Hutchison was a class act and for a period of time it looked as though he could help United on the greater things.

Don Hutchison (Sheff United & Scotland)

Kendall moved back to his old club, Everton, and soon came in for his former player, taking Hutchison, to the other Merseyside club for a fee of £1,000,000. He was a player who Sheffield United would have been prudent to have held on to.

Len Allchurch born in Swansea in 1933, was the younger brother of, the great, Ivor Allchurch. Both played international football for Wales. They played together for their home town club, Swansea, until Ivor was involved in a high profile transfer to Newcastle United. Len was soon to emulate his brother and play in the top division.

Sheffield United were facing a final push for promotion and decided Len Allchurch was the man to do a job down the right flank. A transfer fee of £12,500 was agreed and Len became a Blade in March 1961. With only eight league games left and having just lost to Ipswich, the eventual champions, United needed a final push. Allchurch certainly gave United the surge they were looking for. He scored six times in those eight games, four of them being the decider. Not a bad return from a winger. United finished fifth in the league in 1962. Allchurch played in 39 league games scoring eight goals. He also played in 12 cup games as United reached the last eight of both major cup competitions. Season 1962-63 was to be a carbon copy for Len, with 39 games and eight goals, but United had to settle for a mid table spot. The trickly little winger saved his best season at the Lane until he was in his 30s scoring ten goals in

Len Allchurch (Sheffield United & Wales)

33 games in season 1963-64. His next and last season was blighted by injury and he only made four more league appearances for United. He was transferred to Stockport, were he won the Fourth Division Championship. He ended his league playing career back at Swansea and gained another promotion in 1970. He finished his footballing career, at Haverford West, once again playing alongside his brother, Ivor.

Colin Morris was made in the traditional winger mould: beat a man, get the ball in towards goal and let the strikers do the rest. He could beat a man with either trickery or pace and weighed in with an average of above one strike in every four appearances, not bad for an out and out winger.

Morris came to United near the end of their Fourth Division campaign in 1982. He played 23 games scoring four goals and probably setting up another 30 for Edwards and Hatton. He was Ian Porterfield's final piece of the jigsaw that won the Championship, with United scoring on 94 occasions.

Colin had started his league career with Burnley but soon moved on to Southend and then Blackpool. It was from Blackpool that Morris was signed for just short of £100,000.

Morris was top league scorer in United's return to Division Three and managed to score 20 league goals in season 1983-84 when United gained another promotion, this time to Division Two. He was a regular in the side for the next few seasons until Dave Bassett

Colin Morris (Sheffield United)

came along and sold Morris, who was then 35 years old, to Scarborough, a team he later managed.

A side note about Morris - he holds the record for most penaties scored and for most missed.

John Tudor was another player who did not appear in the Red and White of Sheffield United for many games. The cold statistics are 64 league games with a return of 30 goals, not a bad record. He played for three seasons and appeared in 19, 24 and 21 games respectively. All his appearances for United were in Division Two.

Tudor was born in Ilkeston, Derbyshire in 1946 and played his early football with Coventry City. Sheffield United had Tudor watched and decided he could do a good job for them leading the forward line. He signed for United in 1968 when only 22 years of age. United hoped this new signing would give them the kick start they needed to help them gain promotion back to the First Division.

At the end of Tudor's third, and last, season the Blades did gain the promotion they had been searching for.

John Tudor never actually appeared in the top division for Sheffield United. He was transferred to Newcastle United early in 1971, when he was swopped for ex Wednesday striker David Ford and goalkeeper John Hope. Tudor would have been a good player to hang on to. With John playing alongside Dearden and Woodward, United would have had a formidable First Division attacking force.

John Tudor (Sheffield United)

As it was Ford was a bit of a disaster with only two goals in 21 appearances and Hope, after a good start, was never going to be the replacement for Hodgkinson. Tudor went on to a fine career with Newcastle United playing alongside Malcolm MacDonald

S h e f f i e l d

Fred Priest played 246 league and cup games for Sheffield United and scored 86 goals.

Alfred Ernest Priest as he was Christened is one of only a small number of men to hold a League championship medal won by Sheffield United in 1898. If the League only gave medal to players who had played over six games then only 12 medals would have been issued that year, the only time the Blades have ever won the Championship.

Priest made his debut for United in September 1896 and scored the only goal of the game against Burnley. He went on to score another 10 goals that season, making him the leading scorer for United. The following season, when the Championship was won, Fred played in all but two of the league games. He, also, played in all three FA Cup final for United, two wins, in that halcyon period between 1899-1902.

A player who could be relied on for the big occasion as well as scoring important goals, he managed 18 FA Cup goals in his career at United.

He moved to Middlesborough in 1906 and then joined Hartlepool as player manager in 1908, staying there for seven seasons. He kept the Market Hotel public house, in Hartlepool, until he passed away at the very early age of 47 in 1922

Fred Priest (Sheffield United & England)

Fred Furniss made his debut for Sheffield United in a wartime game in 1941, against Everton. What makes it a slightly different blooding to most debuts was the anti aircraft gunfire and sirens sounds that could be heard in the background. They played the game through an air raid.

Fred Furniss was a Bevin Boy at a local pit and when old enough joined the Army. He still managed to turn out for the Blades on numerous occasions. Making 116 wartime league appearances. He was a member of the 1945-46 Football League North Championship side.

Including his wartime games, Fred played over 430 games for Sheffield United and scored on 18 occasions. Fred was noted for his speed and attacking play. This was unusual in itself because playing at the back in those days actually meant just that. An attacking full back was not a regular sight on English grounds. Furniss won a Second Division Champions medal with United in 1952-53. For the last three seasons at the Lane, Furniss battled with Cec Coldwell for the right full back spot: it was a battle royal. Obviously, the younger man eventually claimed the shirt. Fred joined Chesterfield then Worksop and when he could no longer sustain a semi professional career he carried on playing in local football leagues until the age of 55.

Fred Furniss (Sheffield United)

Ted Hemsley will probably be the last Sheffield United player ever to play professional football as well as play full time county cricket on a regular basis.

Hemsley was signed from Shrewsbury Town, a club were he had made over 230 league appearances.

Arthur Rowley had just been appointed as the new Sheffield United manager and his first job was to go back to his old club and sign his old club captain, Hemsley.

Ted went on to make even more league outings with United than he did with Shrewsbury. He appeared in 247 league games as well as 28 cup matches.

In his first season, Hemsley struggled to keep a place in the side and he must have feared the worst when Rowley was sacked. Thankfully, it was John Harris who took over the club reigns once again and he gave Ted his chance at left full back.

Hemsley, thanks to Harris's help, had found his true position and he made it his own for the next six years.

Ted Hemsley (Sheffield United)

Hemsley was an integral part of the promotion side and performed equally as well in the top division. In fact Ted Hemsley was voted The Supporter's Player of the Season in 1973. Ted was given a free transfer to Doncaster Rovers in 1977 and continued County Cricket until 1982.

Simon Tracey made well over 300 league and cup appearances for Sheffield United.

Simon started his career at Wimbledon and was reserve for a few years to Big Dave Beasant. After Wimbledon's FA Cup Final win over Liverpool, Beasant was transferred to Newcastle United and Simon Tracey stepped in, his first game being the Charity Shield at Wembley. Unfortunately, it was a reversal of the FA Cup final result with Liverpool winning 2-0.

After a few games for the Dons, their ex manager, Dave Bassett brought him to Sheffield United for a fee of £12,500.

Simon always had to battle for the goalkeeping position, firstly with Graham Benstead, then Phil Kite, Mel Rees and finally Alan Kelly. To actually manage as many games as he did is testiment to his goalkeeping prowess.

When Sheffield United gained promotion, in season 1989-90, Simon played in all 46 league games. United finished second to Leeds United on goal difference. A fine goalkeeper and an excellent servant for many years to Sheffield United.

Simon Tracey (Sheffield United)

Brian Richardson was a hard man, at least that is how he was perceived by his opponents and most of the opposing fans. He was a tigerish tackler and determined in every aspect of his, mainly, defensive, game.

Richardson was an all round sportsman, playing football and cricket for Sheffield Boys and going on to be signed as an amateur by Sheffield United in 1952 when only 17. He took three years to break into the first team but by 1957 had

became a fixture of the famous United defence that included Hodgy, Coldwell, both Shaws and Gerry Summers. That back six played together as an almost unbroken defence unit for six years. Within that period United gained promotion back to the First Division and so nearly achieved a cup final appearance, in 1961, only to fall to Leicester at the second replay of the semi final. Whilst that sound defence was in place the Blades reached the last eight of the FA Cup in four successive seasons.

Richardson was slightly underrated by the fans. Their total reverence of Joe Shaw, Hodgkison and Graham Shaw, the latter two gained England honours in that era, perhaps overshadowed the work Richardson, Coldwell and

Brian Richardson (Sheffield United)

Summers did. But it must be said he was an equal part of the cog that made up that brilliant back six.

Brian Richardson played for the last time for United on April 24th, 1965, playing in 35 league games that season. Brian was sold by John Harris to Swindon for £3,000 in January of the following year.

Stuart McCall was born on 10th June 1964 in Leeds. He made his Football League debut for Bradford City in season 1982-83 when only 18 years old.

He made his Sheffield United debut some 20 years later aged 38.

Stuart McCall is one of soccer's superstars. He has played full international football for Scotland, played in the top flight of English and

Scottish football appearing in both national Cup Finals, as winner and runner up.

He has appeared for top sides such as Everton, Rangers and Bradford City. He was voted Bradford all time greatest player in a poll of fans.

He has scored well over 60 goals from a midfield position as well as being transferred for well over £2,000,000 in total

To some Unitedite's his signing was not seen as a good purchase, too old was the cry. He really proved them wrong with two very strong seasons playing over 30 games in each. His experience rubbed off on to Tonge, Jagielka and Montgomery an imeasurable contribution to Sheffield United's future. His two seasons also saw United play in FA Cup and League Cup semi final games as well as reaching the

Stuart McCall (Sheffield United & Scotland)

Millennium Stadium in Cardiff to face Wolves in a play off final.

Stuart is now assistant manager at Sheffield United.

Stewart Scullion is not a name that springs instantly to mind when compiling a list of star players who, over the years, have worn the red and white stripes of Sheffield United. Stewart was bought from Watford in 1971, when 25 years of age, to replace Gil Reece. He played a big part in the newly promoted United side which had finished second in Division two in 1971-72 season. The Blades managed a very respectable tenth place with Scullion playing in 36 of the 42 League Division One games possible and scoring six goals.

He was a speedy, tricky winger with good ball control and had powerful shooting ability with both feet. He could get the ball across from both wings with amazing accuracy. These crosses helped Dearden, Woodward and Currie all reach double figures in league goals.

Unfortunately, Scullion was injured early the next season and only managed 13 games and even fewer the following season, only playing four games. So with a record of only 54 games and just seven goals he was released by Ken Furphy.

Stuart Scullion (Sheffield United)

Stewart was sold back to Watford perhaps a little prematurely by United, but, to be fair, they did have Tony Field starting to shine brightly.

After Scullion had another few seasons at Watford he plumped for the lure of North American Soccer. Scullion played for Watford 344 times and scored 55 goals.

Nick Montgomery is a young midfielder who was born in Leeds on 28th October 1981 and 18 years later signed for that other big Yorkshire side, Sheffield United.

He made his debut, seven days before his 19th birthday on Saturday, 21st October 2000 as a sub in a 4-2 defeat at Norwich City.

Still only 25 years old, Nick Montgomery is well on his way to 200 games for Sheffield United. In his six years at the Lane, Nick has averaged about 30 games per season. His duties are of the defensive stifling nature, therefore his goalscoring is on the low side, only seven managed to date.

A player who was sometimes underrated by a part of the crowd, he battled through to become a player who most Unitedites want as a permanent fixture in midfield. His 'never say die' attitude is the thing that will always win over the fans and Nick has certainly done that.

Another product of the youth scheme he has gained recognition at Scottish international level and if, as expected, Sheffield United step up to the Premiership it would further enhance his chances of gaining a place in the Scottish side that will try to qualify for the European Championships in two years time.

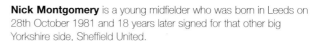

Nick Montgomery (Sheffield United)

Sheffield

The Managers

In the ten years from 1889-1899 Sheffield United did not have a manager as we know the term today. In that period the cricket was overseen by John Beckett Wostinholm and the newly emerging football team was concentrated on by Henry Herbert Stones along with his trainers and captain.

When Sheffield United merged as a cricket and football club in 1899 the man in charge was John Nicholson. He had been the secretary of Attercliffe Football Club and assistant secretary of the Sheffield and Hallamshire FA.

His title, at the club, was Secretary and he would take advice from trainers, team captains and the like, within a committee format, but he was in overall charge of Sheffield United for 33 years. Sadly, Nicholson died in 1932 as a result of a road accident.

In 1932 Teddy Davision was appointed manager of Sheffield United. Although Davison had been a fine player, a goalkeeper of England international class, he was an ex Sheffield Wednesday player. This did not go down too well with some of the fans, especially after United were relegated for the first time in their history in 1934, only two years into Davison's managerial time at Bramall Lane.

But Teddy slowly gained the fans respect with a FA Cup Final appearance in 1936 at Wembley, sadly, losing 1-0 to the Arsenal. Promotion followed in 1939 and to add to the fans' enjoyment, they pipped, local rivals, Sheffield Wednesday by one point for that second place.

United fans will also be in his debt forever for signing Jimmy Hagan from Derby County in 1938.

Davison was in charge at United all through the Second World War and brought cheer to fans by winning the Football League North title in 1946. He suffered one more relegation and then in 1952 decided to retire and named his successor, Reg Freeman.

Freeman had been a player and then manager at Rotherham United for over 20 seasons and was well respected throughout the game. His first season in charge was what every manager must dream about, he guided United to promotion, as Champions, back to Division One.

After a struggle to survive in that first season back in the top flight, he managed mid table respectability the following year. Sadly, for Freeman and Sheffield United that was his last act in charge. Before the new season started Reg was taken ill on a pre season tour and passed away, aged 61.

In 1955, Joe Mercer became the managerial replacement for Reg Freeman. This was a position that was filled rather speedily so as to have someone in place for the beginning of the new season. Mercer came to his first managerial job directly from leading Arsenal to every trophy possible. So it was perhaps a little too much to ask of him, as a new manager, to understand the problems of a struggling club. His first season saw the team relegated. Mercer, himself, admitted he made mistakes, but most of his new signings worked out and he gave debuts to some excellent long term United stalwarts. After three seasons Mercer was given the opportunity to manage a First Division club and he jumped at the chance. Joe later managed Manchester City, to FA Cup, League Championship and European Cup Winner honours. He also had a stint as England manager in 1974.

The next man into the Bramall Lane hot seat, 1959, was John Harris, another ex player who had played at the top level. Harris captained Chelsea to their only Championship title - that is until Russian Billionnaire Abramovic came on the Stamford Bridge scene and bought a trophy or two!

Harris was a tee total, non smoker who did not swear. You wonder how that went down with his new charges? Good or bad points aside Harris did the job. In his second season, United gained promotion and reached the last four of the FA Cup, losing in a second replay to Leicester City. Harris became the longest serving post war manager with Sheffield United giving 13 years' service.

In between Harris's two stints as manager, Arthur Rowley came in for one, rather unsuccessful, season, 1968-69.

After John Harris was finally replaced in 1973 a merry go round of managers came and went in quick succession.

Ken Furphy, lasted less than two years. It must be said he did guide United to sixth place in Division One but the following season started poorly, only winning one out of eleven games played and was sacked in October 1975.

Jimmy Sirrell, the new manager, came in with United positioned at the bottom of Division One and could do little to move them up the table. United were relegated with only 22 points gained. Tony Currie was sold in a bid to ease financial problems. Sirrell like Furphy lasted as manager for less than two years. Now United found themselves next to bottom place in Division Two. Sirrell was sacked on 27th September 1977.

Harry Haslam was next on a managerial treadmill that seemed to be going only one way. After nearly three years and facing relegation, Haslam was replaced by World Cup winner, Martin Peters.

Peters could not avoid relegation and being the manager who took Sheffield United down to the Fourth Division for the first, and thankfully, only time in their history was enough to inform the ex West Ham player his future lay outside football.

Ian Porterfield came to the the managerial post in June 1981 and took United to promotion as Champions of Division Four. Within another two years he had gained them another promotion, this time taking the Blades up to Division Two. Strangely, in Division Two, a malaise seemed to settle over Bramall Lane, especially in season 1985-86, and the team and supporters lacked any spirit. Porterfield's contract was terminated and from January 1986, United's youth team manager, Billy McEwan, was put in charge.

McEwan's stay at the helm also lasted less than two years. His policy of blooding young players was proving a worry and relegation was looking possible. After a horrendous home defeat to Oldham Athletic, 0-5, in January 1988, McEwan resigned.

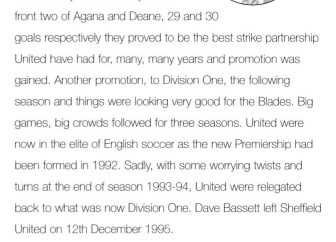

Enter Dave "Harry" Bassett. His first challenge was to get United away from the bottom three positions. In that particular instance, he was not up to the job and United were relegated. The following season, 1988-89, was a totally different story. With a front two of Agana and Deane, 29 and 30 goals respectively they proved to be the best strike partnership United have had for, many, many years and promotion was gained. Another promotion, to Division One, the following season and things were looking very good for the Blades. Big games, big crowds followed for three seasons. United were now in the elite of English soccer as the new Premiership had been formed in 1992. Sadly, with some worrying twists and turns at the end of season 1993-94, United were relegated back to what was now Division One. Dave Bassett left Sheffield United on 12th December 1995.

An even faster, managerial, merry-go-round started: Howard Kendall: December 1995 until June 1997 – Nigel Spackman: June 1997- March 1998 – Steve Thompson: July 1998 until November 1998 – Steve Bruce: July 1998 until May 1999 – and Adrian Heath: June to December 1999. The longest serving of these five was Kendall who was in charge for 18 months.

December 1999 until the present. Neil Warnock now manager at Bramall Lane is a self confessed Sheffield United fan through and through, Neil has led United to some excellent times. Hopefully, with another few to come including promotion to the Premiership.

Sheffield

Teddy **Davison**

In season 1932/33 Teddy Davison was appointed to the position of Secretary/Manager of Sheffield United. He came from a similar job he held at Chesterfield. This was a decision that did not please all the Bramall Lane fans. Davison had been a Sheffield Wednesday player for many years. Teddy steered United into 10th position in Division One.

Davison's second season in charge would be the worst in United's history. They were relegated, finishing bottom of Division One. Even a league double over Wednesday could not console the fans.

A mid table placing in Division Two left fans still unsure of Davison abilities. His signing of Ephraim 'Jock' Dodds on a free transfer from Lincoln helped his cause a little. The young Scot scored 19 league goals in his 28 appearances.

In season 1935/36, Sheffield United managed third spot, in the Second Division and it was their successful FA Cup run which, possibly, cost them a place back in Division One.

A record crowd of 68,287 saw the Blades beat Leeds at Bramall Lane in the fifth round, then defeat Fulham, 2-1, in the Semi Final. Sadly, a Ted Drake goal gives Arsenal the cup in front of 93,384 fans at Wembley, although a Jock Dodds header rattled the crossbar.

The next two seasons saw the Blades possesing the best home record in Division Two but they still have to settle for seventh place and third respectively.

In season 1938/39, Sheffield United secures promotion to Division One, finishing in second place, beating Wednesday into third by a single point. Davison, a very astute manager, paid a small fee of £2925 for a slim 20 year old from Derby County – Jimmy Hagan.

Sheffield United managed just three games when the outbreak of World War II suspended the league. A Regional League was set up and United finished third in the East Midland Division.

Davison stayed in place at the helm of Sheffield United

throughout the war years and in his 12th season steered the Blades to the Championship in 1946, albeit, the Football League North.

During those war time seasons, Joe Shaw, who went on to make the record number of appearances for United, was given his debut by Davison.

After the war with the old leagues restarted, United finished in 6th position in the top division. Davison's signing, Hagan, was one of five forwards who scored into double figures.

After finishing in mid table security in 1947-48, no one really expected United to struggle to avoid relegation the following year. Unfortunately, after a home win against Blackpool, United went another 15 games before another victory. These statistics, along with United only gaining three points from the final six games, condemned the Blades to bottom spot in the First Division and relegation back to Division Two.

United were denied promotion back to the First Division by a goal average margin of .008. This hurt Sheffield United, especially as it was Wednesday who were promoted in second position behind Tottenham.

In the following year, 1950-51, Sheffield Wednesday offered a British record transfer fee for Jimmy Hagan. This was turned down by player and club. The season petred out with United only managing eighth place in Division Two.

Season 1951/52 saw Davison and United finish 11th in the Second Division. The season will be best remembered for the record 7-3 victory over Sheffield Wednesday.

Now 65 years old, Davison decided he should step down as manager and he suggested Reg Freeman (ex Rotherham player and manager) to be his replacement. Sheffield United agreed and Freeman was appointed the new manager. He brought instant rewards to the club by claiming the Second Division Championship.

Teddy Davison passed away in February 1971 aged 82.

Sheffield

Joe **Mercer**

Joe Mercer was born in Ellesmere Port, Cheshire and the first team of note he played for was Ellesmere Port F.C.

Mercer played at left-half and was spotted by Everton who took him to Merseyside in 1932 at the age of 18. Joe claimed a regular first team place at the beginning of the 1935-36 season. His game was built on powerful tackling and having good anticipation of the opponent's next move. Mercer made 186 appearances for Everton, scoring two goals and winning a League Championship medal in the 1938-39 season.

He gained five full England caps during his time playing for Everton FC. Sadly, as with most players of his era, Joe Mercer lost out on seven years of football due to the Second World War.

He was in the army gaining the rank of sergeant-major. Mercer still managed to play in 26 wartime internationals, many of them as captain.

Mercer, during the wartime period, was maligned by the Everton management about his effort in a game and although he he consulted a doctor and had a knee operation, for which he had to pay himself, there was bad feeling between player and club.

A little disillusioned with Everton, Mercer was transferred in 1946 for £9,000 to Arsenal, although he continued to commute from Liverpool.

Joe Mercer quickly became captain of the Gunners, and won an FA Cup winner's medal in 1950 and League Championship medals in 1947-48 and 1952-53.

Joe retired in May 1953, but changed his mind and returned to playing duties at the Arsenal for the 1953-54 season. After breaking his leg in two places in a match against Liverpool, he was forced to retire. Mercer played 275 times for Arsenal, and was voted Football Writer's Award Player of the Year in 1950.

After Joe had retired from playing, he started to look around the leagues for a managerial post to pursue his ambitions.

Sadly, Sheffield United manager Reg Freeman, died in the close season before the 1955-56 football term had started. Although a tragic time, the Blades had to find a replacement, quickly. So, in August 1955, two days before the the first game of the season against Newcastle United, Joe Mercer was appointed.

The new manager did not get off to a brilliant start. His pedigree with Everton and Arsenal as a player counted for nothing in his new job. He lacked hands on experience and in his first season Sheffield United were relegated.

He was still learning how to man manage and deal with players less skillful that the ones he was used to working with.

Now whilst Mercer never achieved anything of note at Bramall Lane, he did buy some excellent players and he brought together and coached the defensive set up of Hodgkinson, in goal, backs Coldwell and G Shaw and a half back line of Richardson, J Shaw and Summers. That group of six was to serve Sheffield United better than any other defence in their history. For this reason Mercer is selected as one of the five best managers to be in charge at the Lane.

United did spend the next three seasons in the Second Division, but never finished outside of the top seven places. In his last season 1958-59, they finished in third place.

Mercer decided in December 1958 that he wanted to move to a bigger club. He resigned and moved to Aston Villa who were bottom of the First Division. He suffered relegation to Division Two for a second time.

He built a good young side at Villa Park and the team became known as the 'Mercer Minors'. He led Villa to victory in the first League Cup in 1961, a two legged affair, but was then sacked in 1964 .

Within a year Joe was back in management and he went on to enjoy success with Manchester City between 1965 and 1972. During his time there, City won the First Division (1968), FA Cup (1969), League Cup (1970), and European Cup Winners' Cup (1970) - A glorious three year period.

He later managed Coventry City from 1972 to 1975, during which time he was asked to be caretaker manager of the English national football team after Sir Alf Ramsey's resignation in 1974.

United

Sheffield

John **Harris**

John Harris was born in Glasgow, during the First World War, in 1917. His father played for Newcastle United and it was obvious with his talent and his father's connections within the game that young John would become a professional footballer.

He plyed his trade with Swindon, Swansea, Spurs, Wolves, Chelsea and finally Chester City where he was employed as player-manager. His longest spell was at Chelsea where he won the League Championship in 1955.

In 1959, after three years in charge at Chester City, John Harris, became the new manager at Bramall Lane. United, now a top Second Division side, had a very sound defence. This was a Mercer legacy.

Harris guided United to third and fourth positions respectively before, at his third attempt, he gained promotion in season 1960-61. They finished one point behind Alf Ramsey's Ipswich Town.

Harris's next season saw Sheffield United gain fifth position, in Division One. This had not been bettered since before the Great War, in season 1906-07.

Harris continued through the early to mid sixties with a youth policy that saw the likes of Mick Jones, Alan Birchenall, Bernard Shaw, Len Badger, Alan Woodward and Barry Hartle start to blossom. With the old rearguard defence still doing a sound job, all seemed well.

Season 1967-68 gave Harris some warning signs when the team found themselves into March before securing their first away win of the season, against Fulham. The sale of Jones and Birchenall, early in the season, was committing football suicide and after nine years, with one promotion and a run of decent league placing in Division One, relegation once more beckoned for Sheffield United.

Harris stepped away from the helm in season 1968-69 and allowed Arthur Rowley to try to steer United back up to the top

flight once more. Rowley only managed 9th place in Division Two and wasn't allowed any time to build the side to his liking. After one full season he was sacked and back came John Harris. To give Rowley credit he did buy Eddie Colquhoun, Dave Powell, John Tudor and Ted Hemsley. All of these players went on to become firm favourites with the United fans.

It has to be said that Harris was never a man to gamble in the transfer market. He would bring youngsters through the system and only very occasionally delved into the transfer system, generally bringing in lower league, low priced bargains. It is said that he had Jeff Astle and Kevin Hector both recommended by his chief scout Archie Clark. This was before either had made the moves to bigger clubs or gained England recognition.

Back at the helm, Harris got back to what he did best: guiding the team with the youngsters he brought through the ranks, as well as the experience players that Rowley had purchased.

It all went wonderfully well. The captaincy was given to Colquhoun, who relished responsibility, and the team simply gelled. Promotion was gained and United had three more seasons under Harris's leadership, all in Division One, before he moved up the Sheffield United ladder to the post of Senior Executive.

Harris had a period in 1977 when he became chief scout for Sheffield Wednesday.

John Harris died in Sheffield in 1988

United

Sheffield

Dave **Bassett**

Dave Bassett didn't quite make the grade as a top class footballer. He had trials at Watford and Chelsea. The response from both clubs was disappointing and he did not receive a further invite. His best efforts to break into league football had failed so he moved into non-league football with Walton and Hersham. He gained a FA Amateur Cup winner's medal as player in 1973, when Walton beat Slough Town 1-0 in the final.

In 1974 his displays attracted the attention of the Wimbledon scouts. Wimbledon, at that time, were playing in the Southern League. The 'Dons' went on to win that league's Premier title in the next three seasons and were duly elected to the Football League in 1977. Dave Bassett played 35 League games for Wimbledon FC before he retired, becoming the club coach, in 1979.

He became manager of Wimbledon in 1981, and in that first year led the Dons to promotion up to the old Third Division.

Regegation the following season was a real bitter pill for Bassett and Wimbleson. After having four consecutive years being Southern League champions and gaining two promotions it seemed as though the bubble had burst.

As a manager, Dave Bassett was now to be tested. To prove his ability he lifted the Dons and went on to win the Fourth Division title in 1982-3. The following year Bassett's Wimbledon finished runners up in the Third Division and gained promotion again.

In 1984, Dave had a week of madness when he left Wimbledon to take on the manager's job at Crystal Palace, then changed his mind and returned, within seven days, to Plough Lane.

The ultimate goal was achieved, when in 1985-6 Wimbledon won promotion to the old First Division, and in that first season in the top flight they managed third place.

He did move away from Wimbledon in 1987, when he took the helm at Watford but it was an unhappy stay for him and in February 1988 he joined Sheffield United.

Dave Bassett came into Bramall Lane with a new broom and swept away a lot of what he perceived as the drab old Sheffield United. He sold players, some who were still crowd pleasers, and some he thought could not do the job he wanted. Within all this turmoil United were relegated.

Season 1988-89 saw Dave go back to Watford to buy Tony Agana, who he paired, up front, with Brian Deane. That was Bassett's masterstroke. The goals flowed from this pair and with Bassett giving Sheffield United a higher profile, the whole place seemed more vibrant. With 59 goals from the front two, United gained promotion.

Another promotion, the following season, was gained with Sheffield United just losing out on the title, through goal difference, to Leeds. Both teams gained 85 points. In just over two seasons Bassett had taken United, with two promotions, up to the top division.

United played in Division One for two years and finished 13th and 9th. The following season, 1992-93, the First Division was renamed the Premiership and United finished 14th in the new league.

The following year was a devastating-one for the Blades. Not one of Bassett's players reached double figures in goals and the circumstances in which they were relegated on the last day is still a mystery. Accusation of cheating and match fixing were levelled.

Dave Bassett stayed another full season, when the Blades finished 8th in Division One, before resigning on Dec 11th 1995. He needed a new challenge, and so he returned to Crystal Palace.

Bassett's stay at Palace was short and in February 1997 he joined Forest to help player-manager Stuart Pearce with his administrative duties. The duo of Pearce and Bassett could not save the club and Nottingham Forest were relegated in May 1997. Pearce resigned and Bassett assumed full control of first team affairs at the end of May 1997.

The following season was to be a great one for Bassett and Forest, winning the First Division title and promotion back to the Premiership in May 1998.

Striker, Kevin Campbell was sold (without Bassett's knowledge) and the other front man Pierre Van Hooijdonk decided he no longer wanted to play for the club going on strike for three months. By Christmas, Forest were bottom of the Premiership. They never regained any real form and were relegated. Bassett was sacked, January 1999. He was appointed manager of Barnsley in June 1999. After a brief stay he did TV pundit work and also had a spell at Leicester City.

Sheffield

Neil **Warnock**

Neil Warnock was born in Frecheville, Sheffield, on December 1, 1948, and has been a supporter of the Blades for most of his life.

Neil Warnock started his football life playing for Swallownest Miners' Welfare and Sheffield Club in the local leagues around Sheffield.

He was spotted by the scouts at Chesterfield and his career in league football took off.

After he left Chesterfield he moved to Rotherham United, Hartlepool United, Scunthorpe United, Aldershot, Barnsley, York City, and Crewe Alexandra. It has been said of Warnock that he has had more clubs than Jack Nicklaus.

As a player, Neil was an industrious forward cum winger who served all of his clubs to the best of his ability. Sadly, he was never deemed to have the skill that First Division sides are always on the lookout for and had to display his talent in the lower reaches of English League Football.

When his days were numbered on the pitch, Neil decided it was time to take a look at the managerial side of the game.

He started his managerial career with a six month stint as player manager at Gainsbrough Trinity. He soon moved on to Burton Albion in February 1981.

In 1986 he moved to Scarborough who were in the equivalent of what is now the Conference and he gained promotion to the Football League in his first season.

He then went on to manage Notts County and after two promotion play off wins at Wembley he took a struggling third division side straight up to the top flight, Division One. His reputation was growing, but he had a slight disagreement with the Notts County Chairman and moved out. After a brief spell at Torquay he took the reigns at Huddersfield Town and then went to the south coast to manage Plymouth Argyle. He was to be in charge of two more clubs, Oldham Athletic and Bury, before reaching his current position at Sheffield United.

Throughout his time as manager of the aforementioned clubs he contested four play-off finals. Unbelievably, all of them were won and promotion secured. He gained two promotions, as mentioned with Notts County, and once each at Huddersfield Town and Plymouth Argyle.

These are things that are well noted in the boardrooms around England and he was asked to become manager at his home town club, Sheffield United. How could he refuse? Neil Warnock was appointed to become manager of the South Yorkshire side in December 1999.

It must be said that to take on Sheffield United at that time was a brave decision. Steve Thompson, Adrian Heath and Steve Bruce had all been in charge within the last 12 months. Although United had managed a respectable 8th place in Division One, they were 38 points behind the Champions, Sunderland, but only 23 above the relegation places.

Warnock with only a shoestring budget in his first few years managed to develop a skillful team.

In 2003, Warnock led Sheffield United to the semi-finals of the FA Cup and League Cup as well as the final of the First Division play-off. In doing so United defeated premiership sides Sunderland, Leeds and Liverpool. Losing to Arsenal in the FA Cup Semi Final was a hard pill to swallow as United were the better side on the day.

More difficult to understand was the play off final against Wolverhampton Wanderers when it must be said United did not seem to be on their game in the first half and the Midlands side ran out 3-0 winner. Funny old game, football.

During December 2005, Warnock was offered a very lucrative position at Portsmouth, but he refused in favour of staying on at his beloved United.

With a brilliant beginning to the season, 2005-2006, when it seemed Sheffield United were unbeatable, we now have to endure the worrying climax of the final few games to see if Neil can gain another promotion by taking United up to the top division in English football.

Neil Warnock is the sixth longest serving manager in league football as this book goes to press.

My father was born the year before United last won the FA Cup in 1925, and my grandfather was born the same year United last won the League Championship, 1899.

As you can see from those dates it is a long time since the Blades won a major trophy.

My father, Joseph Liversidge, started to watch Sheffield United in 1930 when his older brother, Harry, took him to Bramall Lane for his first home match.

He saw the end of the 1925 FA Cup golden era of Gillespie, Johnson and Tunstall. The rise of Jimmy Dunne, a record goalscorer, United's first ever relegation, the signing of the legendary Jimmy Hagan. He also saw Bramall Lane's John Street Stand, in December 1940, flattened by German bombers. On that same night, in Mountain Street, Attercliffe, my father's own house was bombed out of existence, leaving him and his family homeless. They were rehoused just off Ecclesall Road, behind the Star Cinema, so going to see United play became a little easier. By 1941 my father had joined the Royal Navy and did not see many more matches for the next few years. He did, though, see United lift the wartime Northern League Championship in 1946, just before the reforming of the old league system.

After leaving the Royal Navy, my father courted and married Joan, my mother. I came along in 1949. Six years later in 1955, he took me to Bramall Lane for my first ever football match. It was the last game of the season and United won 5-2.

For the next few years I went with my father to the games played at Bramall Lane on one Saturday and then Hillsborough the following weekend. He would not let me go to the away games as he deemed me too young. When I was 14 years old I was allowed to go away on the supporters' coaches. I started to follow Sheffield Wednesday to their away games and became a lifelong Owls supporter. I even took my pregnant wife on to the kop when Wednesday were relegated on a very wet evening in 1970.

Six months later my wife gave birth to a son, Mark Richard Liversidge, who was persuaded, by the time he was six, by his grandfather to be a Blade. Mark along with school friends Rory and Phillip used to watch United on a regular basis and went to as many matches as they could afford. They managed to see United at Wembley and the Millennium Stadium in their semi final and play off games. Sadly, those homeward trips were filled with dejection.

His job as a betting shop manager dictates he can no longer go to Saturday home games, but he occasionally gets the pleasure of working within Bramall Lane for his employers.

So, armed with some of our memories and my father's recollection of the older players, we have chosen the players who epitomise Sheffield United, from the greats who won every conceivable honour to the odd player who just caught the fans favour for a moment in time. Not all are internationals or record goalscorers. Some are just players who arrived did a good job and went their way. Some of these players stayed for decades others a season. See if you agree with our choice of the greats!

Gary Mackender has superbly illustrated some of the Sheffield United players through a 108 year time span, from William (Fatty) Foulke (c1898) through to Paddy Kenny (c2006). He has also captured some of the many strips that Sheffield United have worn over the years.

Abby Currier has illustrated the managers and, even though she had never heard of some of them, made an excellent job of capturing the men who were at the helm of the club through the good and sometimes bad times at Bramall Lane.

Acknowledgements

I would like to thank my father **Joseph Liversidge** and my son **Mark Liversidge**, who gave me their time and memories of their favourite Sheffield United players;

Sheffield United Football Club, and particularly **John Garrett**, Sheffield United Hall of Fame, for his invaluable assistance;

Eric Brodie for his generous help with some of the older pictures of the Sheffield United players;

Stephen and Jonathan Bradley for their help with reference material to back up our descriptions.